Scenes That Sizzle!
Contemporary Dramatic Monologues
for Women and Men

Joshua Brylsteen

NMD Books
Simi Valley, CA

Visit our Web site at http://www.NMDbooks.com.

Library of Congress Cataloging-in-Publication Data
Brylsteen, Joshua
Scenes That Sizzle!

Includes bibliographical references and index.
ISBN: 978-0-9706773-3-4 (Softcover)

1. Performing Arts - Theater   2. Acting & Auditioning
3. Arts & Entertainment

First Edition March 2010

Performance Rights and Royalties

The scenes and plays in this book can be reproduced
in limited quantity for scene study, audition or
educational purposes.

Any use of the works herein for paid admission is
subject to a standard royalty fee. For permissions and
royalty information, please write to:

NMD Books
2828 Cochran Street
Suite 285
Simi Valley, CA 93065.

Acknowledgements

I wish to thank the following theaters and individuals for their help in preparing these scripts for public presentation:

The Stella Adler Academy, Hollywood; The Sanford-Meisner Center of North Hollywood; The Actor's Studio, New York; Mr. James Lipton for his kind guidance and support, Garry Marshall and the Falcon Theater, Burbank, Tim Robbins and the wonderfully supportive members of the Actors Gang; the late Mr. Lonnie Chapman and performing artists at the Lonnie Chapman Repertory; the honorable Mr. Martin Landau for his generosity of spirit; James Karen and the many other actors, writers and theater directors that helped make this book possible.

Forward

Theater is without a doubt a labor of love and those who work within its magical bounds are a special and courageous breed. Few suffer more indignities and hardships, and still fewer prosper.

Despite its difficulties, the theater is the greatest art form mankind has ever devised, and I believe the monologue is the greatest of its many artistic expressions.

These monologues and scenes were developed as a means for adult actors to use in auditions and workshops, seeking to tackle roles which contain a wide range of emotions and which challenge their skill set in an imaginative and creative way.

They were developed and performed at theaters and workshops throughout the Los Angeles area.

Although written as adult roles, they can be used by actors of any age, sex or ethnic persuasion, despite the character descriptions which accompany them, however, this recommendation comes with one caveat: some of the language and the thematic content of these plays and scenes are of a highly adult nature.

I would also like to make mention of formatting script conventions. There are many different ways to format the play script, and in some cases these sides were re-written as teleplays, movie scripts and radio scripts, so there are some differences in the conventions, such as italicizing parenthetical stage directions in some, and bracketing same in quotes in others.

As the saying goes, 'The play is the thing.'

Enjoy!

JB

*"Though this be madness,
yet there is method in't."*

- from "Hamlet" by William Shakespeare

Table of Contents

Voodoo Moon / 119

A welfare mother living in the projects of Chicago uses voodoo magic to kill her husband, then to rid her neighborhood of drug dealers. (A Monologue)

Waiting Room / 135

Two suicide victims find themselves trapped in a limbo between Heaven and Hell, forced to play a most demanding game of Russian roulette. (A two-character One-Act Play)

The Switch / 189

Two brothers - One a death row inmate and the other a prison guard, meet in the death chamber of a prison to confront a life and death crisis in which only one of them will emerge alive. (A two-character One-Act Play)

Cadillac Highways

(Spotlight on the lone crumpled figure of Clifton J. Tibbs, a surreal and rather curious personality whose ageless features and intense gaze transfix all who enter his orbit. He removes a dirty crumpled cloth hat from his head, walks to the edge of the stage and squints out into the darkness, addressing the audience.)

CLIFTON TIBBS:

(Happily)

My name is Clifton J. Tibbs. I've been called a world traveler, a transcender of time, a scribe, a sage, and even a bit of a visionary. How I came to attain this humble level of stature at this juncture of my existence is a complete mystery to me.

For anyone who has ever felt alone and lost in the world, and had trouble finding their way, my story will come as a true revelation. My passing trough your lives at this moment may be attributed to the glories and mysteries of the universe and my travels over the back roads and byways of this great country, and the people I encountered. My story is the story of the Cadillac Highways, how they changed my life and how I came to discover truth and meaning in the very heart of America.

I must warn you that my strange and remarkable tale contains truths that are more fantastical than any fiction. What happened to me in my journey was to change my life forever and in the telling, it may change yours, for what I am about to relate will challenge your beliefs and your outlook on the great mysteries of life. What happened that was so significant it changed my life forever? Listen and you shall see.

(Clifton places the hat on his head, pivots, and takes his place stage center. After a moment of reflection, he begins his story.)

My story begins, as many stories do, at an ending. I was a middle class husband, in a middle class suburb, with a middle class wife and two middle class kids. I was bored shitless and scared out of my mind that I would lead a life of quiet desperation and die in obscurity, the secret fear of the struggling writer. Mary Jo didn't understand that an artist vibrates at a different intensity than say, a Harry, or Sid, or shmoe down at the office.

She nagged and she yelled and she did what many women end up doing to their men once they're roped and branded and in the corral, presumably for life. She became the dreaded she-bitch-from-hell and made my life a living nightmare. She found out that living with a writer was not the perfect Barbie and Ken life that she or her mother had envisioned for her. I finally decided that to live in their prison was a lie.

(Sincerity)

But how could I leave them? They had come to depend on me as I had come to depend on them. I loved my kids, and even though my love for Mary Jo was dying, I still felt responsible for her.

(A confession, difficult to admit: fear)

The truth is, I was also afraid.

Afraid of what I might find out there, just beyond the periphery of my view; afraid of what might happen to my kids if I left them; afraid of the loneliness I would feel without them.

It was a dilemma of the highest order. Was I staying in a situation I despised because I was afraid for me, or for them?

(Strength, resolve)

But, I decided, as many great explorers historically have done, that to turn away from truth out of fear was to live in a self-imposed prison.

I needed to find out what it meant to be free, and why my heart longed for the open road.

Mary Jo and her family had placed me exactly where they wanted me, and I had placed myself where I thought I should be.

Change would have to happen, whether it came easily or not. And, much as the forging of steel would have to be done with the use of muscle and heat, so would the elements of my fears.

To live within the boundaries of someone else's idea of the American Dream was not my fortune.

(With great sadness and emotion)

With great heaviness of spirit, I packed my bags, left a note, hugged my kids, and set out to discover what Columbus had stolen from the Indians.

It was the hardest note I ever had to write.

My true fear gripped me from within. I knew I had to plunge into icy waters and have faith that my spirit would follow where my heart told me to go.

I was still hanging on to the material world and to the things I thought would make me happy. Only in release could my soul be set free, and only in the journey could I ever hope to be truly liberated.

I knew I had only six months to live. It was in that knowledge that I was to live my life to it's fullest.

Being from New Jersey, one tends to head west, if for no other reason than heading east would have required treading water. I packed my copy of William Least Heat Moon's "Blue Highways" and resolved myself to finding America. And, I was determined to do it as far from any interstate road as possible.

(Produces a map, shows it to audience)

You see, on a map, there are the blue lines that show the back roads and there are the red lines that show the main roads. It is my opinion and I share it with Bill Moon, that it's the blue highways that capture the true spirit of the country. I knew I had to find myself and the heart of America, on what I called the Cadillac Highways.

Road warriors reminisce of the days when Route 66 ran through the soul of the country and it's in the memory of Route 66, now gone, that I lay homage to the Cadillac Highways. These are the roads you travel where you can still find flashing neon motels, hamburger cafes, Sinclair dinosaurs, and single screen drive-in movies; where the towns you pass through seem caught in a time warp; Saturday night still means a barn dance; coke still comes in green glass bottles; and juke boxes still have Elvis on plastic 45's.

I knew small town America was dying because its Cadillac Highways were being bypassed by the monolithic stone interstates. But they were still out there, I know, because I found them. And, long after they've been bypassed, and grown over with weeds, they will live on inside each nomad who remembers them. The open road still beckons from the darkness and the romantic lure of adventure and intrigue has never really died. If nothing else, it has grown stronger with our longing for the past.

It was my longing for the past, and my concern over an uncertain future that made me realize I had to break the ties that bound me to my self-imposed prison.

I hitchhiked across New Jersey and over the Allegheny Mountains of Western Pennsylvania. Many rugged men had died to build the PA Turnpike, having frozen through harsh winters, blasting and pick axing their way through the unforgiving rock. I paid homage to them as I caught a ride over the back roads they must have used before the Big Road had thundered through. I young girl at a truck stop restaurant smiled at me and said things with her eyes about sex and having babies and I wondered what ours would have looked like had we decided to try.

I ventured out into the night and walked for miles before hitching a ride with a preacher on his way to Ohio. We drove for many miles without talking and as I looked out through the windshield into the unyielding blackness, I felt fear engulf me like Death's shroud.

It reminded me of the many times I had been thrown into the depths of despair. I had to force myself to move forward. I had to kick at the darkness 'til it bled with light.

The preacher told me someone in Cleveland had seen a vision of the Mother Mary in a Holiday Inn near Lake Erie, and throngs of pilgrims were gathered there as well as news people from three states. He was going in order to ascertain if it was legitimate, as he was writing a book about sightings of the Virgin Mary.

He said, "Son, I've been around the world four times and I've seen visions of the Virgin twice. I've seen her in some pretty strange places. But, when someone says they've seen her in a Holiday Inn in Cleveland, I've got to ask myself are they a charlatan, a devil, or a saint."

I told him there wasn't much difference between a devil and a saint except that one was just crazier than the other. He pulled out a bottle of Old Granddad and offered me a pull. I told him I'd probably had enough whiskey in my lifetime to outlast ten men. He said he understood that just fine and that he knew many that had fallen by the bottle. I told him my theory is that the fall of this country started with the killing of the Indians, and that was done largely through alcohol. He said it was a fine theory, but he'd have another drink just the same.

He winked at me and handed me a faded plastic statuette of Jesus. He said, "Take this, son. It's your own personal lucky Jesus. I stole it off the dashboard of a '66 Impala in a Mexico City Junkyard." He said it had been blessed by a Mexican Angel.

With that, he stopped the car dead, opened the door for me and said, "Step out. Step out over the threshold. And remember, the spirit is with you always and forever. You are a warrior, and your journey has just begun. So, walk in courage, and always walk towards the light, but be not afraid to walk through the valley of the shadow of death." I remember his words and still keep that statue of Jesus with me as I did throughout my journey.

(Reaches into pocket and takes out statue. Use gestures for following.)

As I headed further West, the stars in the heavens seemed to grow brighter and multiply. The expanses of space seemed to broaden. And, by the time I reached the big sky country of Montana, there was no horizon left anymore, only a seemingly infinite sea of stars. It was under this blaze of stars, somewhere near Custer, Montana, I met a cowboy named Frank Forest, who told me about the UFO's, and how they were devils sent by angry Indian Spirits to reclaim their homeland.

Frank had been a rancher for as long as he could remember and one night, in this field, a UFO landed and stole fifteen cattle, making them disappear in a halo of white light. As his eyes sparkled brightly near the firelight, he said, "I watched 'em land and they whipped search beams all over the property, zigzagging and crisscrossing like at one of them big Hollywood premiers. I figured the whole county'd be down here within five minutes. But, nobody ever said they saw nothing."

He said, that night, he'd had a vision, and it was the spirits of Indians, long dead, come to get their due. "How do you know it wasn't just a dream," I asked. And Frank said, "I don't have dreams...anymore. This was a message from the Indians that our ancestors had screwed up, big time!"

He went back into his house, closed the shutters and locked the doors. I don't think he ever looked at the night sky the same way again. To tell you the truth, I know I never did.

I ran into Terri Anne about half way across Montana. She had just left Custer battlefield, having been there because Custer was a distant blood relation, She was honey haired, with big _____ ,

(*Cups his hands beneath his chest, indicating LARGE BREASTS*)

and lips that would make a French whore jealous. She said she had modeled for a skin magazine in California and I believed her. She had the kind of body that I, as a younger man, would have fought anyone for.

(*With great emotion*)

Desire had consumed me. The longing was unbearable. And somewhere past the biological need for release, was the longing for love. It hit me just how much I missed Mary Jo. I could almost hear her voice; the way the touched me; the way she smiled. The grief of her loss was at this moment coursing through me, and I felt the pain of being human once again. Then there was the guilt that I had left them back there, in order to pursue a greater good. My emotions once again, fought to rule my heart.

Terry Anne pretended she cared for me, but she really wanted to hustle me for money. She was a drifter, and her homelessness was borne out of running. She never stayed in one place long enough to form attachments, and she used sex as bait, to get what she wanted. But she also told me she never really enjoyed sex.

We bundled up together in a sleeping bag, under the stars near Custer, and I wondered what it would be like to make love to her. We stared up at the stars, and she smoked a cigarette, while she told me her narrow philosophy.

She said, "Cliff, do you ever think about suicide?" I said, "It's all over soon enough. Why rush it?" "Because life is cruel and miserable and I'm unhappy with the same old shit all the time," She said. I told her, "Then you have to change your view of the world, so at least, you always have something to look forward to. You have to make your own reality. You can't wait for someone to make it for you."

She rolled over and fell asleep, and I don't think she even heard me. Later that night I caught her going through my wallet and pretended to be asleep. Finding nothing, she quietly stole away into the darkness and I never saw her again. I knew there was a lesson in there somewhere, but I didn't know what it was.

I found a roadside cafe off of old Route 66 near Barstow, California, and ordered a cheeseburger. I listened to some truckers talking about the day they shot John F. Kennedy and how the spirit of the country had died with him. I never met JFK, but I remember how he gave the country hope, something to look forward to. This was before Viet Nam, when there was still a promise that we were destined for greater things.

The word about the president being shot spread like wildfire across the land, and a whole country went into shock. I think Don McLean was wrong, and that it had nothing to do with Buddy Holly. Some say that was the day the music died, but I think it was the day they killed Kennedy that changed everything forever.

I reached Los Angeles and saw how it had seduced the great movie kings and cinema queens. The gigantic electric grid that lay below me was alive with dreams.

I spent the rest of the day on a Malibu cliff, staring out over the ocean. I had traveled from coast to coast, and as I stared out into that kaleidoscope of shimmering reflections, came to realize what I had been running away from for so long, was really myself.

There is no true home in the physical sense of the word. The only home is in the heart. If I had learned no other lesson from my travels, this was it. I also found that although a change in geography could change my outlook on my inner self, it would not change me, if I could not stop running away from me. Movement however, did provide the impetus for a metamorphosis. It was also this constant movement cross country and my physical condition that had instilled in me a sense of awe and urgency and I was discovering not only the great distances of this land, but also a boundlessness within myself.

(This is the Turning Point in Clifton's story – his Big Moment)

It was at that moment when release came.

It spread over me like a warm sunset, spread down through me and enveloped me in its glow. As I made my way back across this great land, I felt my attachment to the material world diminishing with each passing mile until time and distance were vague concepts and oneness of my divine connection to the universe became an integral part of my consciousness.

As I traveled my sense of purpose began to take shape with new clarity. But there were still questions in my heart. The experiences I had witnessed on the Cadillac Highways were shaping my realization that my purpose as a physical being had not gone in vain, but it would soon be time to leave this material plane.

Moving back across California, heading east, the ghost town lay fragmented and splintered, in the middle of the Sierra Desert. Some forgotten relic of an ancient gold rush, the dusty burg was now the resting-place for rusty cars and rolling tumbleweeds. As I walked through town, I imagined gunslingers and stagecoaches, and as I looked up at the second floor window of the saloon, I spotted the ghost of a beautiful girl, but I cannot describe her to you here, for it would not be for innocent ears. But, she was the most beautiful thing I ever saw.

(Awe - Realization)

As I left the ghost town, a profound truth hit me. I had been doing battle with myself about being happy for as long as I could remember. I had spent so much time and effort trying to acquire material things, I'd never occurred to me maybe I was wrong.

(Turn, posture deep in thought, resume stance)

My journey back across the country was marked by the ghost of a Civil War soldier. He told me tales of the war, of the rebuilding of the South, and the endless pleasures he'd experienced in the loving arms of many a Southern belle. He had haunted the halls of a Mississippi plantation since his death, after the war, had lost his way, and drifted across the plains, in search of some unknown entity. He spoke of Lincoln, and assassins, of hard whiskey and riverboats. And, in his tales of barbershop Saturdays and ice cream Sundays, he confided in me that the secret to finding true happiness with a woman began with finding a Southern one.

I lost him near the Cadillac Ranch, that monument to the open road, that place where ten Cadillac's lay buried, fins up, in a grain field off of what use to be old Route 66.

The vortex of the twisters on the Great Plains, is like the wildly spinning cone of our existence, turning back in on itself in a never-ending cycle of change.

Loren Eisley once wrote that man is merely the product of the ooze from which he sprang – a host of untold desolations. I felt this as I headed back across the country, under the starry skies, past the billboards that once held the motorist captive on the road to Burma Shave.

I returned to my point of departure only to find that Mary Jo had packed, taken the children, and left. She had left a note saying she wouldn't return and had left the matter of the house for her brother to handle. I walked away from the house and wandered for hours knowing that I had left my past inside those walls long ago.

Time is a continuum, having no linear beginning, middle, or end. The magic and power of the universe had been there all along for my discovery, only I was too blind to see it. The only true prisons we have are those we construct around ourselves. I had reached a point of critical mass way back on that road with Mary Jo, and now the time had come to release it from my life.

The journey was not only that of geography. It was also a movement toward enlightenment, a state of mind-a spiritual awareness.

All the spirits of all the people who had ever lived and died seemed to live within me now. Every shred of knowledge of the Earth and the universe became one with me and I was filled with light.

(Happy again)

My children would grow up healthy and strong, and find their own way. Mary Jo would find another man, and I would continue my journey out on the open road, another ghost of a wayward traveler.

I would meet up with other entities, those long ago dead, and exchange stories of the road and of other lives I'd led. Their dreams, memories and reflections were part of the psyche of man, the collective body of knowledge that mystics and seers have drawn on since the dawn of time. Now, mine were added also.

I drifted high above Salem that night, and floated Westward again. I know that the open road was where I really belonged, and that discoveries were still out there, waiting to be made. My physical body died that night, before the altar, and with it, all the sufferings of the flesh.

So you see, what you have before you is not the man, but the spirit, a timeless energy that never diminishes. For life is energy and energy never dies. It merely changes form.

(Remove hat. Step forward to address audience.)

That seems like eons ago, but is only a sliver of my realm of experience. I returned to my origins with the sword of truth and I've carried it with me ever since.

Life goes on in a never-ending cycle of birth and rebirth, and we are all but fuel for the continuum of this constant flow of energy. I discovered that the living of life to its fullest is its own greatest reward.

My spirit could now be set free.

I found this in the heart of America, on the magical, wayward star paths of the Cadillac Highways.

CURTAIN

The Judges

A stark, minimalist stage, antiseptic white. There is no furniture but for an empty chair in the center of the stage. It is illuminated by a pale circle of white light.

Seated at the chair, erect and motionless, as if in a trance, is the regal figure of Andrea Krassner. Her hair is a matted, tangled mess, her face ashen. Dark circles beneath her eyes, she looks like she was hosed down and put away wet.

She is dressed in a hospital gown. She still manages to present a stylish appearance. She is strong, possessed of a wisdom beyond her years, a knowledge born of pain. She shields her eyes, trying to focus on an invisible panel of judges that are seated at a long table facing her.

A huge WHITE LIGHT switches on with a metallic THUNK, blinding her like an angry white sun. She holds her hands up to her eyes, trying to peer past the burning light. Her eyes get used to it. She waits some seconds, shaking it off, then addresses the panel.

ANDREA:

You sit there in your stone silence, like the statues at Easter Island, and you took upon me with the shroud of your judgments, and you think you know what goes on inside my head. I know what you are thinking. All you ladies and gentleman of the psychiatric board of this miserable little hellhole they call a hospital. You are thinking why should we let Andrea Krassner back out into the world of reason?

She, a poet of questionable talent, one who paints with the broad strokes of a pen, using the words of great sages from the past, of voices of spirits and ghosts that lived in other centuries, perhaps other worlds? You think on further analysis, she, a nut, pure and simple. For she hears those same voices in her head when everyone else isn't looking.

You who do not know from where these voices emanate, the ruminations of dead spirits long gone?

Why should we release this sick little bitch who says she's seen God? *(laughs)*

Why let her loose on the street to spread her obviously warped delusions onto an innocent and unsuspecting society? (*laughing*) Why should you indeed?

Well, before you pass your judgments, I would like to give you a view of the world from this side of the glass.

And I submit to you that though there is a fine line between insanity and enlightenment, before we are through here today I will prove to you the difference.

Though countless have gone to their deaths under the crucifixion of what they believed. It was not their belief, but what others would have them believe that became their undoing. Just like you are doing to me now.

And who are any of you to tell me I haven't seen the face of god?

For none of you have even come close to the spirit, let alone seen a vision of the divine.

Do any of you know what divine ecstasy really is?

I know what it is.

(her face brightens in fond remembrance)

The faces of the children on the Sistine chapel. Spinoza when he discovered Truth and found a way to write about it. Balanchine when he achieved a full double spiral in mid-air... and it seemed he would never come down. It's that sweet spot theory in time, that second of impossible exquisite agony before the orgasm. That breathless moment before gravity... *(opens her hand)* releases its prey.

It was in the angelic face of my daughter.

(she sits, becomes very sad, begins talking to her as if she's sitting in front of her, she pushes back the imaginary hair from her daughter's face)

Baby, yes, mama's here, I'm okay baby, I'm so sorry I've been away. I miss you so much. Mommy is in a place where she can gather her thoughts. I am writing and painting here, sweetheart, I wrote a poem for you, do you want to hear it?

From darkness comes forth the roar of silence For in the deafening crescendo of that dark There lies the echo of light in timeless space I shall reap your longing in great harvests of truth In wisps of glass falling headlong to their tumbling deaths For all of eternity your heart sings in the shadows abandon And I shall wait for you forever here In these graveyards of shattering light

That was for you honey, did you like it?

No your father isn't here, baby he died a long time ago do you remember? No honey I will never leave you I will be there for you... I will be home soon, and when I get home we can go for a walk in the Cano? Would you like that baby? We can go at night, when it's dark.

All the windows lit up with the blue light of TV screens and people ignoring each other?

Yes and maybe we will go by mister and misses Bickert's and watch them waltz across the living room through that picture window they decorate so nicely at Christmas?

(Her eyes grow wide in terror, as she imagines the child's image fading...)

No! No baby, don't go! Don't leave now, I'll tell you another story, and I'll read you another poem... Heather! Heather...

(Her fear turns to deep sadness, she cries. Eventually, she snaps out of it, and turns her attention back to the judges, great rage and anger building)

I hope you are happy!

You would take away the only thing in my life that means anything to me! Why not just dangle a bone in front of a starving dog? Each one of you should die in Hell! An artist of my caliber, a thinking feeling, perfectly SANE woman with a small child to raise and you would keep me here in chains?

How much of a kickback do you get from the state for keeping me here?

You who steal my work from under me, you've taken my paintings and my writing and you've sold them or placed them in museums, well I don't want to share them with anyone. It is N1Y WORK. I own it, it is of my creation and you have no right to take it from me.

Just like you have no right to take my flesh and blood away from me!

(She calms down. Becomes sad again)

This isn't right. No it just isn't fight. I am a woman of independent means. I had a place on this earth, a place I could go. Raised by my alcoholic father to do the right thing, to not sleep with anyone but him, to treat my mother with respect, god dammit.

When I moved to my own place, my own studio, I met Frank and we were so happy. He and I like lovers in Paris in the Spring, he would sing to me and I would paint and write and we would listen to tapes of Ginsburg and Keats and when we wanted to laugh we'd put on Lord Buckley or listen to the Grateful Dead and we knew our place in the world!

And what did I care he drank more than my father?

What did I care he'd get angry when I was bad and beat some sense into me when I was being a bad girl? Because I can take it. I've always been tough. And I knew not to cry because if I cried I'd knew he'd really give me something to cry about.

Well what the hell?

The spirit is resilient.

It always bounces back, right? That's what makes us so great as a race and as a people. We're tough, by God, and we can spring right back. Dirt... grime... even black heel marks wipe clean with a damp cloth!

Well let me tell you something, you who think you can judge me.

I've seen the inside of the soul. It's there in the middle of your being surrounded by all that beauty. So before you start dissecting me, you better prepare yourself for what you might find.

And it won't matter if you keep me here or you put me out there, I'm still going to be me, and nothing is going to change that. Not Thorazine, not electroshock, not anything you guys can come up with is going to make a shit of difference.

So what are we doing this dance for, this tango of deception across the floor?

Because I am a waste of the taxpayers money.

I can earn my keep out there. I have creative talent, which is more than I can say for any of you.

Look at the lot of you, this looks like the god dammed last supper, all of you lined up at the table with your degrees and your pompous attitudes and your opinions and bullshit theories. Do you really think you understand the human mind? It's like trying to capture an angel on the head of a pin, trying to define black holes or quasars in a universe whose infinity has no bounds!

(She looks to the end of the imaginary table, off *to audience right)*

What about you, Charlie Turnbull?

Two PH'd's from Harvard, a child prodigy, an IQ that's through the roof and you have about as much common sense as an emu in heat. You have no courage, Charlie Turnbull, you are a gutless spineless weasel and without your sheepskins, you are nothing!

(Her eyes move to the seat next to him)

And then there's Doctor Mabel Forman, one of the first black teachers to enter the public school system in an all white racist county in segregated Mississippi. You think you know the meaning of alienation, Doctor Forman? Do you really think the color of your skin qualifies you for a seat in the senate of hatred?

You ought to try being considered separate from the human race awhile, Mabel, see how the other half lives inside the padded room. Try being treated like a fucking vegetable instead of a person with colored skin. I'd trade places with you any day just to watch you swim down here in the snake pit. You wouldn't last a day!

When you look into that manila folder with my name on the tab, that one that sits before you on the table and you see words like "paranoid delusion," "schizophrenic," and "delusions of grandeur", remember my words. Your little units of logic cannot define the intangible.

How can words even describe it? There are no means of communication that can reach beyond the boundaries of your limits to describe the infinite, are there? And so there are no words to even come close to the energy that course through my being at this very moment.

Since that moment I became aware, when the flash came down from the skies and imbued me with spirit, I knew I was one of the chosen ones. The One left standing at the foot of the mountains of blindness, and there isn't a one of you who even has the slightest notion as to what the hell I am talking about.

You think I am a religious zealot, one of those crazy vagabonds that walks the streets and hands out pamphlets to find the keys to the kingdom of heaven?

Oh you are so wrong!

I know what it's like to walk on the jagged edge, a place that's filled with desolation and danger, where demons and angels dance, where apocalyptic visions can give way to heavenly and blissful peace.

None of you can know because none of you are even alive.

You, Charles W. Henry. You drive home by the same route every night and you go home to your wife and your kids and everybody says the same things to each other every night. You eat the same food, you watch the same boring television shows and you don't talk to each other except to exchange meaningless, disposable words.

One day is exchangeable with any other, isn't it Doctor Henry? And when you are dead and gone there won't be anything that distinguishes your life from any other because you were NOT AWARE.

You have no consciousness, none of you! Don't you know there are things in this air, in this room, in this universe that you cannot see, things that vibrate at a different level and if you could just attune yourself to this beautiful sweet song of the cosmos, you might be able to get some spiritual sense of awareness?

But you don't.

Do you wanna know what's more of a tragedy than a woman stuck in a rubber room who shouldn't be there?

It's a panel of so called experts who are book smart but life dumb, who ought to try a day or two in solitary confinement.

Listen to the silence a while.

Listen to the pounding, deafening nothingness that courses through your being like a thousand railroad trains. Listen to it! It's everywhere, it's the sound you can't hear now because you are too busy listening to the incessant raucous noise of your own restless hearts.

But if you would sit in the silence, contemplate on the roar of that silence, you would finally come to point hours down the line, when the locomotives pass, there is only the clean sound of the universe pulsing like stars in a bottomless heaven.

I can hear that sound now.

(Silent for a moment, then she is overcome with ecstasy)

And those seconds that just passed for me were glorious moments filled with joy, with light, laughter and tears of divine happiness.

Those same seconds for you were several impatient moments waiting for a woman who is quite obviously out of her mind to come to her senses.

"A void of boundless space and time

A flutter of light, a shimmer of wind
A vacuum of tumultuous desire springing
to life
On a bed of dark retreat, moving away
from light
Till only dark covers my hidden soul"

"From recesses of torment faceless shift
Layers buried, hidden beneath sands
As in an hourglass, coursing through
years
Eons of dark, again, transgression of
fears"

Do any of you really know what it is to
live, to feel the progress of life through
the fibers of your being?

I don't think so. Because you are dead
inside, you cannot know what it is like to
vibrate at the level of intensity of the
artist, the poet, the lightning rod of LIEFE!

Maybe that's what scares the shit out of
you. The fact I can look at each one of you
and tell you what goes on inside. You play
the game of life, without risk, without
consequence, going through the motions
like marionettes on a string. You take no
chances, unwilling to walk the tightrope,
you cannot feel the course of adrenaline
through your being!

So you go. You visit your dead. You walk among the tombstones and you thank your God on high it isn't you down there with the worms, your bones rotting with the passage of time.

What you don't realize is that you are already dead!

Don't you realize who I am?

I'm Venus De Milo, Catherine The Great, Joan of Arc, every matriarch that ever stood above the maddening crowd to proclaim her greatness, her separateness from the maelstrom of humanity.

But trapped, now you see, in this passage of time. Trapped in this body, in front of you. You who would judge me.

A panel of judges, like you sat before Jesus, and tell me of your narrow philosophy and your rhetoric and lies. Your power plays and your self-serving righteous attitudes. You who would sit before me on your pompous asses.

Hiding behind your theories of behavioral analysis and your psycho-small talk.

Which of you is the Judas?

(She observes them, walking up the line of them like a drill sergeant)

Is it you, Doctor Miller?

Do you really think you can explain away the terrors and madness of the human heart?

How about you, Misses Jacoby?

Can you dissect beneath your mind microscopes just what makes Sammy Run?

What about you, Luckman?

What is the basis for your interpretation of human motives?

There isn't any.

You are faced with me and your theories crumble in the dust, as the pharoes in their tombs and even the great kings that never imagined that one day they would return to the elements. No matter how they tried to preserve their immortality.

You sit there in the illusion of your well ordered existence, but you don't know by what tenuous thread you really hang. You mouth the words to your spouse, your friends, the people you exchange platitudes with. Those who you believe are close to you, with whom you share the illusion of love.

But your words are empty, because they can't convey the loneliness and the alienation you really feel deep down inside. If you listen to your heart, if you clear away the noise in your head, you can feel it.

I promise you it's there, I feel it all the time. I'm feeling it now.

You can't face that, none of you. I don't think there are many who can. Nobody but the mad among us, the artists, the writers, the painters and the poets. We who tune ourselves to frequencies of the insanity that beats at the air like dove's wings.

Well I face it every second in every moment of my life.

All the hours in the day, the seconds pass with time's relentless falling. Sometimes slowly, the grains of sand slipping through the glass. You try to connect with some kind of human feeling, some kind of touch, but nothing can really bridge the gap, the worlds between people.

(She holds her hands out, palms out, touches her thumbs together, making a 'frame with her fingers, an imaginary window)

I see reality through this window. The sun blazes down outside in the yard, it casts brightness and warmth on all Gods creatures, great and small. But darkness, it lurks in the molecules that exist between the brightness of the light. I know because I can see it, and nobody can know what that feels like.

Nobody! *(fear engulfs her)*

To look at the clock and feel the agonizing seconds as they pull and tug at my heart, the heaviness of time's anchor pulling me down to the earth. It seeks to pull me back to the ground, to the elements, to the grave and beyond. It wants to return me to the spinning void of space.

You want to know what it's like to try to make it though all the hours of the day?

Well you can't know!

And then you have the audacity to ask me what do I want?

Well I'll tell you exactly what I want.

I want transcendence from good and evil, this sickening duality that tears at my soul. I want freedom and release from the confines of this madness.

I want to fly, to soar over the heavens with boundless spirit and pureness of heart. To be free of this painful awareness, of the gravity of the body and the anchors of worry that seep over my eyes as ether and threaten me with an ... unending sleep.

To be torn away from the sickness that tears at my gut. The feeling that this well ordered life we live, this seeming rock solid ball of earth is not so solid. What if it were as fragile as an hourglass, and it all exploded in a flash of light, just like it came in?

What prevents matter from imploding in on itself in a blast of energy that would catapult our atoms into oblivion?

The answer to that question is... nothing prevents it at all.

(She jumps up and gets right in their face s)

I realize, watching your faces now before me, contorted with your judgments that you will not grant me the freedom that I want. And if you could but grant me one simple freedom-~ I would be forever in your debt.

To pull all of your energies and just free me of the pain of being human.

(She pauses, for effect, begins to walk toward the door. Then she turns to them.)

If there is any one among you who can do that, then raise your voice in the jubilation of transcendence. *(She looks out at them, waiting, but gets no response.)*

I didn't think so.

(A huge SPOTLIGHT shuts off with a metallic THUNK.)

(She sits in the chair, looks to the ceiling as if she is communing with God, and as she does, the only circle of light which still illuminates her dims to DARKNESS.)

CURTAIN

Time Ballet

(A dark stage, in a shaft of light surrounded by a completely black backdrop, is KARLA LEHMAN, a thin, weathered woman; fiftyish. She appears cultured, yet has the unmistakable aura of a woman who has seen her share of the hard life.)

KARLA:

Late in the evening, as the shadows fall and the night presses its lonely blackness against my windows, I have come to reflect the absurdity and unfairness of life. As a young ballerina I yearned for the stage, the spotlights striking me in mid-leap, the satin shoes and the pirouette, the lean tautness of muscle against leotard. I knew the sweat, the adoration, the applause. Deafening, thunderous rounds of applause, as they lay the roses at my feet. But then, finally, after the audience left, only the empty coldness of the darkened theater remained. I am alone once again, the lights have gone down and I am standing in a pale circle of spotlight. outside of the circle lies an indifferent and terrifying universe, where I dare not venture for fear of leaping into an unknown abyss. I am left with nothing, and I am reminded that I have come into this world alone and will go out alone. The people we share our lives with.

In between are only to comfort us as we wait for our final moments of life.

Growing up in Sparks, Nevada, long before the casinos moved into the desert, I remember playing in the dust. I listened as the planes dropped nuclear test bombs over the gunnery ranges, hearing the voice of my father calling me into the house for dinner. I was his little girl, and I could do no wrong in his eyes. He had always wanted me to be a ballerina. He would set me on his knee and say, 'Karla, one day you'll be a famous dancer, the most famous and popular dancer in the whole world. You'll go to New York, join a company and dance your way around the world.' But somehow, it never happened. My hopes and dreams became sidetracked along the way, the way people's dreams always get lost along the way. When you're busy living your life and there's no time to see how time is rushing by you in a relent-less jet-stream.

Time being called the great healer, I have come to learn that time is not the great healer. It is the great stealer.

My father was the patriarch. His rough, weathered, leathery face showed how the winds of time had ravaged him. He fell victim to the hollowness of the skeptic, and every moment he lived became a great, unmoving weight. He had religion in his soul, then lost it, saying that God was dead and that Jimmy Hoffa killed him. He worked like a dog, my god how he worked He would drive produce trucks across the States, spending days on the road, returning to tell me and my sister stories from his travels. I'll never forget how he cried when they closed Route Sixty-Six. He said 'Karla, small town America is dying.' Just like that, with tears in his eyes, care in his heart. And I thought about that many times, how America is dying, and how I miss the billboards on the road to Burma-Shave.

My mother protected me, never wanting me to be exposed to the evils of the world. She always told me, 'Now Karla, there are bad people, bad men, they will destroy you if you're not careful. Don't be fooled by men, they will hurt you. All they want is one thing, sex. Terrible dirty sex.' So I grew up thinking sex was wrong, the way the Catholics believe. My life was lived under the burden of terrible guilt. There is no guilt like Catholic guilt. My mother made sure of that.

There was a boy I met in high school. Johnny Ziegler. He was a football player, the star quarterback, and he'd taken a liking to me. He offered to take me home in his pick-up truck. Imagine that. I ran home and told my mother and she scolded me, telling me 'You can't go out with that boy. He only wants to use you.' And I cried, I cried for two days. My father came into my room, telling me that mother knew best, and that everything would heal 'In Time.' In time! But it didn't. And there isn't a day that goes by that I don't think about Johnny. There isn't a day that goes by that I don't think about what life might have been like with him. Never a day goes by the clock doesn't tick ever closer to our heals and drives us deeper into the grave. I grew up and married Ben Leaman because I was afraid of the Time Ballet.

We met at the Storey County Fair. He saw me in my summer dress standing in front of the house of mirrors, saw my reflection, and told me I looked pretty, even in the fat lady mirror. I looked into his eyes and knew that my future was with him, a lanky cowboy that reminded me of pictures of my father when he was Ben's age. Ben was a good man. He always treated me and the kids well, even though he was distant. I was used to distance, living out in that desert. A place where distance is a given. In this spirit of Distance, I chose the wrong man to live my life with, but at least I can admit that. Most women could never admit they made a mistake like that. But I did choose wrong, because it was so easy to do. Our lives are affected by those we choose to live with, yet we are so quick to jump that it scares the hell out of me. But I made a fatal jump, and never admitted it to Ben. I was wrong. That much I am certain about in a life full of uncertainty.

Sacrifice, my mother always said 'Karla, you must sacrifice.' There is no sacrifice greater than the ballet life, and alternately, the sacrifice a mother makes for her children. When I was eighteen, I traveled to New York and spoke to one of the great masters of ballet. She showed me what it would take to become a ballerina; the endless days of wrenching grinding work, the physical exertion, the many years it would take. I marveled at the studio, it's shiny wood floors, the dark hues, the stretch bars that lined the walls. I thought of the ghosts that went before me, their bodies pliant and supple with youth, their fresh young faces scrubbed, their hearts pounding, eager and alive with expectant, vibrant life! Their whole lives before them, with nothing but promise and hope for the future. For a short time, I was one of them.

I entered the school upon graduation from Sparks High, my father driving me to New York City in his huge tractor trailer. We drove for three days and nights, listening to Hank Williams on the radio. He told me the life of a dancer would take all that I could give and more. All those hayseeds I grew up with, I'd show them. 'You have to earn your dreams,' he said to me. 'You have to work at making them happen. That's the difference between

the doers and the dreamers in this world.'
Then I arrived at Ballet School.

The girls never accepted me into the fold. I
had entered a twilight world of cultured
dance, charm schools, girls born to families of
old money, ancient legacies. Large homes in
Long Island. Families who raised their
daughters to be poised and pretty and
cultured, to always look their best and to
marry important, rich men. To be a woman of
rank and substance meant to smell good, look
good, and always get a man with a future.
When I entered, I was the black sheep that
had descended on their prim existences.

Do you know what it means to be a loner? I
was always alone, even in a crowd. From the
time I entered kindergarten I knew what it
meant to be utterly alone. When I entered the
playpen they regarded me with indifference,
as if I were in-visible. It reminds me of a
nightmare I had when I turned forty-five ...

(Visualizing)

I am an invisible woman drifting over
gravestones in a cold and wintry world of
half-dead corpses and zombies. Below I see
Ben making love to a dead woman. He is
laughing. As I come to earth I am back in
Sparks, walking down Main Street and no
one ever sees me. The invisible girl that lives
at Six-teen Seventy Seven Larchmont Circle
in Sparks, Nevada, near the gunnery range

where they drop nuclear test bombs on unsuspecting lovers. It was in that desert I learned about aloneness.

How can I shake my legacy of terrible oneness in a cold and uncaring universe? Of wanting and need, the desire for sexual intimacy that is always unfulfilled, the aloneness of it? Feeling if the world only knew my innermost thoughts, they would turn on me, stoning me, driving me away, back to the dead planet where Ben makes love to ghosts of my ancient past.

And so I entered the world of the ballerina, and learned the steps that had to be taken in order to be a part of the dance.

And in my second year of training, I went home at Christmas and Ben said to me: 'Karla. You gotta come home. This is no life for you and I. Not for a local girl. What about a normal life, a life with a husband and kids, a home?' I, being torn down the middle with self-doubt and the cold indifference of New York, eventually broke down. By that Spring, I had taken a bus back to Sparks, back to Ben, back to the beginning, as if the ballet had never happened in the first place.

When I awoke, twenty years had gone by. Two children had grown up and left home, gone off to college, and there we were. Alone. Just me and Ben, left alone with memories of a life that had happened as casually and predictably as manufactured dummies in a department store window. And I, Karla Lehman, was left alone with memories of dreams of a life that could have been but never was.

(Karla dreams)

I am approaching the stage and the announcer is booming: "Ladies and gentleman, the incredible Karla Lehman" But it is not a ballet, it is a circus, and I am a trapeze artist, flying high above the crowd in my silver sequins. I am waving to the glory seekers below, normal people with normal families and incredibly boring lives, people whose wants and desires were different than the realities they are living.

I look down as I swing, and I begin my death-defying high wire act. Their necks are straining, like cranes in a stagnant pond, awaiting in intense anticipation, my daredevil feats. And there is a sexual edge to the danger, like the romantic lure of the vampire, like the attraction some woman have to outlaws and bad men. And I know most of them wish I would fall, for there are spikes below, and there is no net.

(End dream)

What would Freud have said about my dream? That I longed for the danger, living on the precarious brink, as I wished for in my ballerina fantasies? The antithesis of a safe life with Ben, far from the rigors of the road and the harsh uncertainties of fame? Would he have said I had a death-wish, or that I wished to sleep with my father? I would deny none of those things. But deep in my soul I knew the dreams were longings for a life of adventure, romance, mystery, intrigue! In their finality, a longing for a life that never was. But what of all the other housewives I knew in my boring middle-class existence in Sparks? We all lived in identical clapboard houses, watched the same soap operas, had the same routines. The endless laundry.

The perpetual desert heat, the dirt that made keeping the house clean a nightmare. The babies and the diapers and the lost hopes we had in high school. Coffee breaks at the kitchen table at noon. Curlers and bathrobes, Ajax and Clorox, diapers and dreams in the slow tortured process of being broken.

But best of all were our cardboard cut-out husbands, the ones that came home the same time every night and never spoke to us as people, because they themselves were not people. Cardboard cut out husbands and children in a cardboard cut out life. I wished the bombs had fallen on us. Seeing the bombs fall, the walls searing and splitting apart, our flesh leaving our bones, our souls soaring to the heavens.

I remember when my father drove me to New York, we'd be on the Interstate and he'd point out the roofs of the houses that lay on either side of the highway. Held say 'Karla, your mother and I want more for your life than that. A house is nothing but a pile of boards. It's what's on the inside that counts.'

I let you down, Father. I succumbed to the Laws Of Gravity. I found out a house is not happiness. And I never became on the inside what you saw in me on the outside. I managed to hide my true self to the world. My father. In Heaven as he was on earth.

(Laughs)

I'll never forget the day he died. He was laying in the cancer at Sparks General, and he told all of us, my sisters and my mother that there was only one way to get the things you want in life. That's to go out and get them. Then he looked at me, the disappointment in his eyes that I had let him down.

As if to say; 'Karla, you could have been a ballerina. You could have been the best.' And then he died.

I helped my mother go to the funeral home to pick out his casket. The undertaker showed us a casket catalog. A casket catalog! He tried to sell us the American Presidential casket, the model they buried John F. Kennedy in.

He said it is what my father would have wanted. How would he know?

I remember mama, so upset because the undertaker did this, so upset my father died. She was really angry because she felt he had abandoned us, the same way her father had abandoned her, as if it were intentional. I thought that we are all abandoned at one time or another. A life of total isolation, total abandonment. My mother yelled at the undertaker: "You bastard. My husband wasn't a saint, and he wasn't a martyr, and he sure as hell doesn't need your presidential casket to be taken to his maker.' She stormed out of there, past all the caskets neatly lined up for display, and the undertaker looked at me for one impossible moment. I could see he was looking at me in a sexual way.

He was fat and bald and old, but I knew I liked the attention. But all I could do is run after her and try and calm her down. We went to another funeral home and we bought a generic casket for father, one without any names or endorsements of any kind.

His funeral was not an elaborate affair. I realized that I would never see him again, and that there was no road back to him ever again. That life could be so short and death so final brought me to understand that life is but a Time Ballet, ever short, sometimes sweet, a difficult lonely struggle, a dance with death that ultimately ends in our parting quickly from the material world. What lies beyond is an intangible mystery.

I have come to reflect upon this mystery of death. The Egyptians claimed life sprung eternal, that the passage of the soul was merely a transitional device that we would all return here in life of some form. We are but changelings, only to return in different form. I am not certain of this. All that I am certain of is the certainty of death, and its seeming finality.

(Dreaming)

I am facing an empty curtain and as it rises, the orchestra bellows its mighty fanfare, the heat of the lights on stage blazing alive. In the rush of applause, I am swept off my feet by a strong and sinewy dancer, lifted high into the air, held aloft like a baby in a father's arms. In that moment, I am in my father's hands, as he looks up into my eyes, he is laughing, bouncing me, talking to me. I am secure, happy --- so incredibly happy --- The stage is alive in the choreography of the ballet, the sweeping, fluid movements. The orchestra is weaving a tapestry of sound that seems as if it could be danced upon itself. I am in heaven.

The dancers swerve and fly around me, a human machine in perfect harmony, sweat, muscle and the law of motion in the dance of the stratospheres. I am thrown into The Light, and as I am thrown, I take flight. I am flying now, high above the stage, past the cables, the sandbags, high up into the rafters, going up, like a crazy balloon out of control, I am growing wings and the audience gasps. I am flying out over the audience now, they are pointing up at me and the ballet has stopped, the orchestra continues to play. I am flying up into the roof vent. Up into the roof vent I go and out of the roof vent, outside now, in the darkness of the cool night I am flying above the city. I am gaining altitude and velocity, my senses reeling from the transformation. High above New York City, the metropolis is ablaze with color! I can see the stars around me, the Manhattan Skyline. The Statue of Liberty at Ellis Island is a breathtaking sight, and I am soaring above her and past her torch.

There is the crash of cymbals, a bright circle of light tears my consciousness and I am now back to earth, back to Life. I am laying in my bed awake, in the darkness of my bedroom, staring at the ceiling, wishing and hoping for things that never were. Ben is beside me, snoring. I turn to him and I say 'My god, Ben. To think I've shortchanged you. I never really wanted motherhood as much as I wanted The Dance. I never wanted you as much as I wanted to be in the spotlight. I never wanted to sell my soul to the Devil of Boredom. You may ask, what is wrong with normal, what is wrong with Boredom?

If the world were full of people who wanted to be famous, it'd be like living in Southern California anyplace you were. But I leave no answer for him. Knowing the plight of the artist, the outcast, and the vagabond. I am all of these things and more.

Was it by a divine plan that life has come to be a Time Ballet? For me, it is as if a shadow had fallen across my life, and I was destined for this chasm. Even when mother died, right here in her bed in Sparks, dying of some ageless thing they never found a cure for, I felt like the curse had been passed on to me from mother to daughter. This was the curse of life, the shadow, which hangs over those who seem marked for misfortune. It is a legacy I pray I have not left for my children.

From the time we are born we juggle the elements, trying to do battle with the laws of gravity, the hands of the great clock ticking relentlessly away at our hearts. The juggling continues throughout our lives, throwing the balls into the air and hoping and praying we will be able to keep them moving without dropping them.

Without losing our sanity. The world clips by at an incredible warp-speed, becoming more complicated with each moment. We are spinning and turning wildly out of control until it is going so fast we yearn to get off. If one by chance should lose their way, the way back to the beginning is lost.

So where has this Time Ballet left us in this cold and indifferent universe? Has our presence here made a difference, and if so, to what magnitude? I have left behind my only legacy and that is my children. I have chosen what my life was to be and lived with it, and now, at this juncture, I can only surmise that it be the best I could give.

When I walk among the tombstones and see the littered yards of lives that once were, I wonder, did they make a difference, or were they all just human product, the result of some romantic tryst? Have I made a difference? I do not know the answers to the great questions of life. But I do know its pain.

And what of Ben? Was he merely a conduit through which our children passed? One night, quite late he turned and looked at me and saw me stargazing a million miles away, and he asked me if I cared. If I cared? Was it that obvious that my flights of fancy had taken me further and further from reality? My dream states had overcome my waking states and the path to san-ity obscured. In this madness, I laughed about becoming normal. What was 'normal?' Something I never really was.

When a person has a different way of looking at the world people around them avoid them. A traitor in the ranks. They always called me weird. 'You're weird, Karla.' They saw me as strange, but I was no different from them, deep down inside. They were all talking about me behind my back. I was quite sure of that. We learned in science of animal behavior when a new breed of animal hits the jungle, all other species move out of its way. Maybe Darwin was right, and that's why the dinosaurs never made it. There is an aura which surrounds us, and that aura contains within it the essence of what we are. For some blessed with beauty, it creates a gravitational pull which brings personal power and sex. For the ugly ducklings not blessed with great legs or breasts to back it up, we are left with our solitude. As a young girl I used to spend summers at my aunt's home in Cape Cod, walking the rocky shoreline. I watched star-crossed lovers hand in hand. They were always engaged in some secret intimacy, a closeness I never understood.

I was always a voyeur on the outside of this intimacy, wishing I were down there with the man, wishing I had been with him when he be-stowed the magic of his touch on me. I would watch the lovers on their towels and blankets, entwined so tightly, surrounded by the sand and waves, and I would dream... Dream the terrible loneliness away, my mind in some romance novel where men never beat their lovers, where women were always ready, and fantasies always came true. It was with these thoughts I realized that life was never ideal for the less pretty among us. Life was always a struggle for emotional survival.

There is a price to pay in the process of natural selection for the less well endowed of face and body. Which is why I needed to achieve, and my obsession with dance.

How far could I have gone in the ballet before fate had intervened? I dreamed of dancing with the masters. The Russian ballet was in my blood. The New York Metropolitan Opera house would be my home! Traveling from city to city, I would have been the greatest ballet dancer that ever lived!

Could have been ... would have been ... My father always believed you could get anywhere from here if you wanted it badly enough. Did I not—want it badly enough? The memories of my youth haunt me incessantly, until there is nothing left but the past.

The day I lay dying, I remember, the day I left this earth for another place, another plane. I was reflecting upon these things and the moments of my life, the lost loves, the broken dreams. And before I drifted beyond my withered body I recall the brilliant white light. The great light that signifies the departure from this earth, the calling to the great beyond.

I remember the voices from my past, the ghosts long ago dead, the voice of my ballet teacher when she said 'You shall become all that you wish to be, and your journey will take you there.

That was all I remember of that moment, the final moment of my waking, material life. I now realize ... I am ... DEAD!

(looks at herself in wonder)

Dead...

And in this spirit state, I am but a wondering soul, still searching the meaning of my existence. I am but a traveler, and my journey will never be complete, my soul never put to rest, not until the state of perfection is reached. That is the plight of the even the artist, the renegade, the poet and the fool.

I believe I have learned from my past life, as I have learned in my many incarnations before that. Life with Ben was not in vain, I see that now. I have come to the end of this personna. I will go forward to another dimension, another Time dance that may see the great dream fulfilled. I will then begin again, at the brink of a new dawn. It is there I will become a part of the continuum.

It is there I will embark upon the beginning of this and yet another ... Time Ballet.

CURTAIN.

American Gothic – Forward

This is a theater piece that was written for three actors to play on the same stage together, but is actually three separate monologues. Three members of a family have been killed in a car accident, and their ghosts are now standing in a limbo dimension, each telling their own version of their family story and how they came to their untimely end.

American Gothic

There are three figures on the stage. KENNETH ATKINSON: a middle aged man, EMILY ATKINSON: a middle aged woman, and their teenage daughter, SHELBY ATKINSON, 15. They stand perhaps three feet apart. They are eerily motionless, a weird, unearthly look in their eyes. The spotlight illuminates only Shelby, who stands in the middle between them.

SHELBY

My name is Shelby Atkinson. And it was I that kept this family together, right down to the bitter end. Had it not been for me, it would have crumbled long before it did. Shelby Atkinson, the monument. The cornerstone to the patriotic duty of keeping your ass above water when the waves crashed too high.

I don't remember the exact moment our nuclear family unraveled, or even what caused it. It all seemed so right, for so long. To our immediate neighbors, we looked like the healthy, quintessential all -American family. Dad had a great job, Mom worked on her book, and me, well, I was busy being a teenager. There were soccer games, and barbecues, drive in movies, and family photos at K-mart. But something had crept across the carefully manicured lawns, a shadow, perhaps. Then Trevor died, mom started drinking, and Dad began to look at me like I was the main attraction in a titty bar. So I guess is the nature of desire, to want something you can't have, or to long for an ideal that exists only in your head. But to attain the object of your desire means you can't want it anymore, so that want is replaced by yet another desire.

What was really strange was that while Mom and Dad and even myself began to change, we didn't notice it. We just kept on playing our roles like we were in some Saturday morning cartoon, oblivious to what was happening to us inside. How did I notice there was even a change?

I think it was Mom's poetry, which was getting weirder with each passing day. I mean, you don't go from writing sonnets about flowers and bees one day, and then the next you're writing free association with decidedly gothic overtones. She started becoming obsessed with the darker side of human nature, and her verse got, well, pretty gruesome.

And Dad wasn't much better, either. At first, he was a real family man. But as the months went on, he started spending more and more time on the internet. I think he got hooked up with some lunatic fringe group out of Michigan that dressed up like soldiers. He talked about them sometimes, late at night sitting alone in front of his computer. He said they were preparing for a war, something about a race of super blacks rising up and enslaving the white supremacists.

My attitude toward Dad didn't get any better when I found naked pictures of fifteen year old girls on his computer, hidden in a spreadsheet file. There were even a few pictures of boys in there, which really gave me a different perspective on ole dad. But it was all getting pretty twisted with him, too. But he never saw it.

As for me, I started reading more and more books, and the more I read, the more I think I understood. But with the knowledge of the ages came not only a sense of elation, but a neuroses born of the creeping realization that we were all hanging by a very thin thread. Not just mom and dad and me, but everybody.

I, too, was going out over the edge of reason, beyond the realm of my own perception. It was probably akin to what the ancients experienced when they had a religious awakening.

These stirrings in my heart I could not explain, but they were there. It was for the want of love and not knowing quite how to get it that lay at the heart of the matter, I was pretty sure of that. I'm not talking about the love that the boys in school wanted to give me, that was more of a Darwinian thing, the need to procreate with a desirable female. No, I was talking about the essence, the purity of love, and the longing that it created in men's hearts. The destruction that it caused when it mutated. And it does mutate, but why I wasn't quite sure.

Just like a cell, healthy and strong, then something inside goes haywire when the sun hits it a certain way. It starts spinning madly out of control, making copies of itself and turning in against itself till it devours its own, and then there is the mass cellular destruction that results in death. The death of the sun and stars, the end of the innocence, the death of the heart.

Sorta like my mom and dad's love for each other. It went from a storybook dream to the depths of some tortured hell. And once mom started writing lots of poems about death and dying, that pretty much killed their sex life.

(she pauses for a dark moment)

Their transformation was a Kafka-esque journey into a dark abyss, and I had a ringside seat.

But in a lot of ways, their transformation was a mirror of my own genesis into the void.

(fond remembrance)

but there was a time when we were happy, all of us. We went for those long drives in the car, a sport utility vehicle, and mom pointed to the trees as they changed color outside our windows like some beautiful Monet, and the sun that shone on her face made her look so pretty.

Dad called her his great ballet dancer, cause she used to study under Balanchine. That was long before the spirits took her looks. Dad used to say that, the spirits. It was the same spirits that stole the souls away from the Indians and left them dying and drunken on the plains.

What he meant by the spirits was the Seagram's. I remember the smell of it in the liquor store, you could smell it right through the bottles. A dark musky, sour scent, the unkempt promise of sex with God.

You could smell it on her, the sour mash seeping through her pores like stinking rotten formaldehyde, and you smelled it, no matter what she did. When she drank it she became the martyr for the ages, and my father had to bear the burden of every imagined infidelity that had ever occurred to every woman since the dawn of time.

And the only thing he had ever really been guilty of was staying with her, because by staying with her he was in league with the devil and he didn't even know it. He had engaged in a deadly tango with insanity. Which is a very big price to pay when you're not getting laid in the process.

(a faraway, strange smile)

I remember their faces at the end, the lights flashing through the windshield, the slam of brakes and the deadly hiss of airbags.

(laughs)

The look on my dad's face was sublime pleasure at the moment of impact, like he knew we were gonna die. I think they both knew.

And my mom? I looked over at her just before the crash. That sick bitch.

There were waves of ecstasy rippling her face, between the flashes of horror. I swore she would have had an orgasm, had she had time. But she didn't. She was getting off on knowing my dad would never have another woman... and then... her time...

(snaps fingers)

...was up. Just like that. I don't even believe for a moment she was thinking of me.

...It was I who kept this family together.

The next spotlight illuminates only EMILY ATKINSON. She's middle aged, we can tell she was pretty once, but her face shows the etched lines of alcoholism.

EMILY ATKINSON:

Don't believe a thing that little bitch tells you. I fought like a saint to keep this family together, God knows I did. I've felt like a rock of Gibraltar from the beginning. Had I not kept Kenneth's pants and shirts pressed and hanging in perfect formation in our closet, he could not have kept his job. Had I not forced Shelby to read Byron and Shelley and Whitman, and instructed her not to fold the corners of her pages to bookmark them, well it's doubtful she would have made it to the tenth grade. And if I hadn't kept those boys out of her jeans, I'm sure she'd have at least four illegitimate children by now. Not all them white.

By the time she had reached fifteen years of age, she had grown into quite a piece by then, surely with little genetic help from Kenneth. She'd inherited my ass, my tits, my good looks, and my grace and charm. And were I not there to keep her raging hormones in line, the whole thing would have tumbled like a house of cards in a windstorm. She would have ended up a tramp on the street, you're goddamned right she would've.

(laughs)

I was the matriarch, yes I was, and I don't want anyone to forget it. But when the neighbors bring up the subject of Trevor, well I just pretend it never happened. I'd tell them, just go on about your business,

now, and never you mind about the boy.
And if they pressed the issue I'd tell them

(*shouting*)

I don't want to talk about it! What
happened to Trevor is none of your
goddamned business.

(*calm now*)

To hear Shelby tell it, I was a screaming
demon from hell. Just the sort of thing
you'd expect from a little bitch. Chalk it
up to the ranting of a rebellious teenager.

Oh but shit she reminded me of me, when
I was her age, all spitfire and fury, ready
to ignite the world. And I swear by the
blood of Bobby Kennedy I could've made
a difference. But then came the Vietnam
war. And we shouted and we picketed and
we lobbied our congressmen until they
could no longer ignore our voices. But
after twenty thousand soldiers died in the
face of our protests, our voices were but
ghosts on a lone mission into purgatory.

Of course I drank. Who wouldn't if they
were faced with pressures I had to deal
with every day.

Living with an idiot for a husband that
couldn't think for himself. Living with a
daughter who thinks that hip-hop is really
music. It's fucking identity crises, that's

what it is. Of course I drank. Who wouldn't? But my own daughter makes me out to be a drunk. I'll have you know I could drink any man under the table, and that includes Barney Holloman. Now there's a lush if ever I saw one.

He'd be under the table and puking, I'd still be out on the dance floor, showing every one of those losers how it's done.

And don't think I never noticed them looking at my body. There wasn't one man in any of the bars I hung out in that wouldn't have paid a weeks salary just to sleep with me, and that was well into my forties.

But I'd never do that. I was always too much of a lady for that. And I can tell you I had much better things to do with my time. Like writing, and I'm a damn good writer, too. And who gives a shit I never published? What fucking difference does that make? When I'd finish American Gothic all the publishers and editors and critics, they'd see I was a talent to be reckoned with! It would be my crowning achievement!

I could see all the reviews that would have run.

(indicates headlines with her hands)

'MODERN DAY POET REDEFINES LITERARY EXCELLENCE - BLOWS ESTABLISHMENT AWAY' or even 'AMERICAN GOTHIC SETS THE NEW STANDARD FOR AMERICAN POETRY.'

But I never had a chance to finish it. I was too busy keeping my family together to write, and god knows I needed booze every now and again just to help me cope. Inspiration would come, someday.

(sadness)

But it wasn't to be. They took me, before it was time for my defining work. The work that would set me apart. The work that would explore the inner depths of the human soul, and it's mad embrace with death. So it was to be the ultimate irony it would be death that would prevent its completion.

(far away look)

The disintegration of our family? Why, it never happened. I don't know what that little bitch was talking about. We were a happy family, all the way to the end! I made sure of that, and even when I was dying inside, when every sense of my being was clouded with despair and self-doubt, I kept my head held high. I never let on to either of them that I was falling apart.

What had caused my inner turmoil? It was the knowledge of the secret, that's what it was. The secret that was mine to keep. That we were all falling, tumbling down deeper and deeper into the mineshaft. And that creeping suspicion we'd had that there were demons in the darkness waiting to take us. The secret knowledge that all those thoughts were true.

But they never suspected, not my family, not for a moment. I would not allow them to see even a moment of weakness.

So up came the armor I needed to construct around myself to prevent myself from being pecked to death by life. My grandmother used to tell me that life's problems were like little chickens, and they'd peck at you with their tiny, sharp beaks, tearing at you piece by piece. One small peck wouldn't hurt you. It was the thousands of small pecks that would leave you a bleeding human wreckage, dying in the dirt.

I wouldn't let them get to me. Not Emily Atkinson.

I was a like a film director on the set. When the problems came up, I vanquished them one by one, nipped them in the bud, head on, without even losing a beat.

I was Catharine the Great, on the battle lines, walking into combat. Of course I drank. Who wouldn't of? But I was never an alcoholic.

But I sure as hell needed something to deal with those idiot editors. What the fuck did they know about *poetry?* They sit there at their tidy mahogany desks with their banker's lamps and their voice mailboxes and their primary corporate objectives. They're publishers, for Christ's sakes, they're not writers. What did they know about sitting alone in the dark and facing their demons while the great blank white stares them back in the face?

They sit on their asses ninety floors up in their glass prisons and look down on God's grimy creation. We, the sweaty little worms who churn out their pap day after day grinding it out while the editors look down their noses and attack us with the razor edge of their marking pens.

And at five o clock they ride their elevators down to the street and get in their cars and ride to their mansions on Long Island, their cocktail parties and their social graces. Their moral fucking imperatives.

And where are we? In front of the great white, night after night, putting our terrors down. And they hate us. They hate us because we can write. Because we have the courage to sit in a empty room and put it down for the rest of you to see. Fucking editors.

Try baring your soul every hour of the day and raising a family like I did. Without me my family would have died in the gutter in their own filth and decay. So you see, I was their savior. But they didn't see that.

And Kenneth? Please. He was a man once, in his younger days. But he grew accustomed to the pay, to the benefits of corporate life. He got too lazy. He wasn't hungry anymore.

But I remember a time when he cared about a cause. When we marched for freedom, and we flew in the face of convention. His passion was his dream, and our dream was an undying vision for an America that wasn't run by the men with the calculators.

We knew the war was an excuse, a way to make money on the death of our youth. And we cared Oh God we gave a shit about change! We carried the signs and we lobbied the Democrats and we stood up for a cause, God Dammit! But when the war finally ended and the dust settled and we buried the last of the soldiers their wasn't anything left to stand for anymore. And maybe, just maybe, that was the saddest tragedy of all.

(long pause)

But that was many long nights ago. Back when Kenneth had been a man. Fast forward, to the age of yuppie idealism. I had traded my tie-dies and fringes for a more tony, cosmopolitan look. Sort of American Gothic meets Calvin Klein. And I became a mother. Those endless days of diapers and wash cycles, and every core of my being went for the raising of another.

God my little girl was so beautiful. Her eyes had all the innocence of the ages, her mind clear from the manipulation of the marketers and those who would seek public office.

Kenneth would arrive, promptly at five thirty five and change into his Levis and I would prepare his dinner with the precision and dedication of a soldier. Then came the diatribe of how our day went. Both of our endless days of grind and servitude. Of blind devotion to the cause and profit of another.

But I didn't mind. We were happy. We were in love. That was before the shadow of despair had drifted across our paths, and the seconds didn't seem to drag by. When the advent of time's passing was not a heavy weight, in some strange time-dance in a battle against gravity. Before the rains set in on the desert utopian landscape, and before our suburban home became the setting for an American tragedy, the decay of the dream. The death of spirit.

I would hold on to the good times when laughter was only a breath away and in our faces shone the light of limitless possibility.

(light down on Emily)

Lights up on: A middle-aged man, KENNETH ATKINSON, calm, assured, but here is fear behind the façade.

KENNETH ATKINSON:

My name is Kenneth Atkinson. It was I who kept this family together. In the face of all adversity, I stood as a pillar of strength in the storm. And if there was one single thing I could say about my life that made it significant as compared to all the other lives that had come and gone before mine, it was the very fact that my living and dying was of no significance at all.

You could say I fathered a child, and if I had lived for no other reason than to carry on the cause of life, then that would be worthy enough of at least an honorable mention.

(smiles)

All right. I'll give you that. I brought Shelby Felicia Atkinson into this life. You call me a father, but deep down inside I felt my only contribution to life was as a sperm donor.

Of course, there were the financial and emotional contributions. But I never felt fully there, because I never felt fully confident that I was worthy of the title of father and husband. But playing the role of patriarch came easy to me. I'd seen my father do it all his life. I'd had a good teacher in pretending that everything on the surface was all right, but deep down inside the turbulence was grinding away in my gut. You'd never know it but for the Maalox cocktails and the Prozac. My co-workers at the office never even suspected they had a traitor in their midst.

But Emily knew it. She knew it because she was a natural born predator. Her mother had been a socialite and her father had run for the senate and I can tell you that a life of staying on top of the food chain had taught her the skills of survival quite well. The ghost of her parents haunted her till the time her spirit drifted up and away from the wreckage of what our lives had become.

There wasn't a moment in those early dawns when I ever felt confident. Those

Old Spice mornings when I left our home in my clean pressed battle armor of custom tailored conformity that I didn't feel like getting on that interstate and driving into the great wide open.

And I don't think there's a man alive who never felt that way. That maybe all this living from paycheck to paycheck was really just a bill of goods they sold us to keep us in line and coming back for more.

I felt like a factory worker, and the product was life itself, the perpetuation of flesh. The making and raising of babies and imprinting upon them the importance of doing the same.

Even though I was living in the land of the free, I never felt completely and utterly free. I never knew what that feeling would be like, nor could I even imagine what it would be, what form it would take.

So I went off in the morning and dutifully performed the tasks required to bring home the money, while feeling somewhere deep within my being that perhaps all this wasn't right, that it was off balance somehow.

I looked like the all-American family man. Like I'd stepped off the cover of an ad for Gillette. Clean cut, the kind of man you'd want for your all-American family fantasy.

The kind of success-driven man the women watch in the soap operas.

What they couldn't see was that I was falling apart inside. The thread of reason was slowly starting to unravel. And I began to see life and awareness in a whole different way. I thought Emily was on to me. I saw it in her eyes. She learned that from her father. The moment you saw any sign of weakness in a man you slowly circled and went in for the jugular.

She ripped and tore at me with her teeth, but she never drew blood. Her weapon was her silence, her lethal doses of consternation. She shredded my confidence and made me feel like I had lost my own skin. And in a way, I had.

There were many nights just lying next to her in the darkness and while she snored off her drunk somewhere deep in the sheets I'd be staring at the ceiling. I'd see myself rising above our bodies on the bed, and I'd be looking down at the both of us and seeing what a tragic mess was sprawled out on the bed below. Two souls who had once been as One had now fused apart in some cosmic cell division. Then the cells began to destroy one another, enemies though born from the same source. And no two people could have ended up as far flung as Emily and I, like planets catapulted apart in a blind flash that had sent them to far ends of the universe.

As a little girl, Shelby was my lifeline. She was the living image of my immortality. A shining spirit in a storm, she could run to me with her little outstretched arms and embrace the one that had given her life. In those eyes I saw all the light of the ages, a panorama of moving beings. The chain of life, somehow interlocked in a mad spiral of DNA, a whirling dervish of a dance that knew no end. I saw in Shelby everything my forefathers had seen in their own sons and daughters. The cataclysm of spirit and flesh, of chance and happenstance.

The unraveling of the thread had begun at some point in time I could not define. When Emily worked into the small dark hours on her tomes of gruesome imagery. I lie awake at night in the loneliness of our bed, just staring at the ceiling, just wondering what had happened. At what moment had our unity divided us? At what point had the cohesive thread of our understanding snapped in the silence of our blind indifference? When had madness seeped in under the cracks of the door and stolen what had been our birthright?

There was no way of telling, really. I had taken notice of Shelby as a young woman, with her own thoughts, dreams, and fears.

She was no longer mine, she became a daughter of the world. The inevitable chasm between father and daughter widened, and in that abyss, was the very dividing point between man and woman. Her breasts began to grow, her hips to widen, as I fought desperately to block the thoughts I had of her, not as my daughter, but as a young, vibrant woman. I wanted to drink from her youth, to make it my own somehow. But instead of merging I withdrew, deeper and deeper into my own world. I tried to make some sense and meaning of the endless moments and hours.

All the hours of the day when they stretched on into infinity. I sat at my computer and tried to find some solace and fulfillment, but could find none. It was not to be found from catering to the senses. Peace hid at an apex, at the peak of some insurmountable cliff that seemed accessible only to holy seekers and madmen.

So was it the very nature of desire to seek fulfillment but never achieve it, save for trace moments in time? The prospect of such a fate left me in a state of total reckless abandon. I knew what it meant to be lonely. That all men felt this strange sensation of being at odds with the universe. But I had no idea that it would creep into my heart and conquer me so completely.

It wasn't anything I could quite put my finger on, but rather something that lurked at the outer periphery of my vision. A monster in the shadows. I couldn't talk about it to anyone, not to my friends, and certainly not Shelby. Where had our idealized view of the American dream led us? Down the road to hell!

(laughing)

So I desensitized myself with alcohol and Valium. Not to the degree that Emily had, but to a point to where I could still appear normal to the rest of the world. The guys at the office didn't notice I was different, so well I played the role of responsible corporate man. The pressed white shirts, the Rolex watch. Smiling family photos in silver frames on my desk, and a BMW in the company parking garage.

(his face goes cloudy)

But self-doubt and desire had consumed me. I stood between the civilized world and some primal place in evolution. My thoughts led me to worlds where the cries of beasts and men were indistinguishable from one another. Where law and logic shifted into a realm of survival and stirrings of the dark and deep overtook my longing for release.

I did not know if God or nature governed the thoughts and actions of creatures, but I did know that to deny the struggle would be to admit defeat. Ignorance would not be tolerated by Darwin's Law!

(he goes deep into his pain)

Then came that night. The night of the rains. All of us in the car, heading down that dark and terrible road. The oncoming headlights. They looked like giant white angels, halos, rushing past us in a wash of Van Gogh pastels. It was strange, like a black and white movie with patches of color and fog mixed in, and even the heater couldn't take away the wet chill in the air. All the lights reflecting off the wetness of the black pavement. The headlights rushing past us, stealing glimpses of our faces, looking forward into oblivion.

I cannot say for sure if I turned the wheel away. If I had tried to save my family, or if I had killed them on purpose. Perhaps I could not face whatever outcome was to be as a result of our slow metamorphosis. Of what we had become as a family.

(difficult pause)

Then the lights swerved toward us, catching us in their sites. The sound of rubber against the wet road, the wail of brakes. The awful, inevitable crash. The sound of airbags inflating, the almost simultaneous rip of metal and glass and exploding airbags. The carnage of metal and flesh. The symphony of mortality. An orchestration of our fragility. The breakage of delicate glass stars hung suspended in time.

(great pain)

I am afraid the rest is too difficult to bear. The pain of life has ended.

(pause, with strength)

In the end, it was I who kept this family together.

(He looks outward into the darkness , as LIGHT FADES DOWN ON KENNETH. Kenneth and Emily step back and EXIT, but the audience cannot see this in the dark)

Lights Up On SHELBY:

Shelby stands alone. She reads from a script fastened together by three golden brads.

SHELBY

'American Gothic, by Emily Elizabeth Atkinson. There lies deep within the hearts of men a place where darkness and light converge, and in that place he must reckon with his soul. In that place there lies truth. This book examines that truth in all its horror, and beauty. The passage begins: 'I stand in graveyards unaffected by the ravages of time, sensing and knowing within my being life has passed, then gone, with little to show but the scars of its trajectory. Seconds gone but a mist of scorn, I am a vestige of those who have stood before me here, at the brink of extinction. If dead souls could speak, they would whisper passages of wisdom so great that my ears could listen forever to their rhythms of rapture. And if dead souls could sing, they would sing the sweet song of youth, for it is in their glorious stirrings of days gone by they find their inner meaning. The melody and harmony of all our days as we lived them in the shadow of our younger days. But days pass into nights and youth turns to old age. And we become slaves to our ailing flesh, and long for the days when our eyes shone with the urgency and the vitality of our now forgotten past.

This has brought me to a ghoulish and terrible place , where souls and men drift freely, where desire and madness threaten to keep me in an eternity of stone and steel. This place called...American Gothic.

(She lowers the script to her side, gathers here resolve)

My mother and father had gotten caught up in the machinations of life. Taken from a simple ideal of American sainthood and dropped into the dark dungeon of self-pity and despair. The angst of my mother's descent into hell, her ruin, went unpublished. The Jennerville Sentinel, our hometown newspaper, mentioned in her obituary she had been an aspiring poet of some promise.

My father's passing went largely unnoticed. His position at his company was quickly filled by another, and his days of toil were quietly forgotten. So went the lives of men whose names are inscribed to this day on the headstones of the ancients.

As for Shelby Atkinson, I was memorialized in a small ceremony by well wishing friends and the recipient of a bouquet of flowers on my casket. A small collection at the high school was also taken. These proceeds went to a worthy cause, namely to have "Stairway To Heaven" played at my funeral by Fergie Reingold's brother, who had a folk guitar. It was a closed casket, so the celebration of my demise was not as glamorous as I had hoped.

All of us had lived the lives of a modern day American Gothic. In a twist of irony, we had been allowed some small tear in the fabric of the universe to tell our story, then step back into the folds of history, never to be heard of again.

But in the end, it was I who kept this family...together.

{THE LIGHT GOES OUT ON SHELBY}

CURTAIN.

The Glass House

SETTING: A Bedroom In The White House

PROPS: A padded living room chair, a makeup table and chair, a small revolver (gun), makeup kit, an oval cojee table, bottle of Jack Daniels hay full, prescription pill bottle, crystal goblet, congressional coasters, shoebox of letters, telephone, glass frame with photo of man in it.

Dark Stage. A single spot illuminates ELEANOR WINIFRID STANTON, clad in a bathrobe, without makeup, a raw pillar of life. She stands center stage, addressing the back of the theater, in great, elegant, oratory style, with conviction , grace and strength. She is a pillar of leadership, and brings a slight humor and great wisdom and wit to her opening. Her soliloquy is done in grand Shaekespearian style. She is smiling.

ELEANOR:

It is with a great deal of irony that I, Eleanor Winifrid Stanton, a woman who has lived in the shadow of political intrigue for the better part of her life, should come to her untimely end in a bedroom on Pennsylvania Avenue. Having lived in the phantom shadow of President -Elect Wimbley Foster Stanton as his devoted wife, supporter, and domestic sex slave, perhaps this is not so surprising. Many will come to think of me as a martyr who died for the cause of Truth. But to me, I am a visionary to the cause of personal freedom. A self-appointed sentinal of the glass house, perhaps the only one who has seen through the dichotomy of its power and the transparency of its lies. For "Rule" that was given Life through the media shall die by the media.

The irony is sweet that I should come to my final hour on this earth in a room normally reserved for royalty, heads of state, and a partially schitzophrenic Richard M. Nixon. But it is a fitting point of departure. For it is and always will be the bedroom where the real decisions are made. It is a battle played out on mattresses and sheets, where grenades of false accusations are flung. Or the hiss of that sweet deadly nerve gas of pillow promises left unfullfilled.

(offhandedly amused)

And so, in tomorrow morning's edition of the horrid rag they choose to call the Washington Post, I shall be declared dead. This will come as a shock to the many imbeciles and idiots, charlatans and bums that consider themselves insiders to the great scavenger hunt that is Washington.

But for the few who have seen through the smoke and mirrors of deception and rhetoric, the ones who know this is ...all... just a glass house, it will come as no surprise at all. To those senators and the pages who kneel down before their Gods in zen-like devotion, perhaps no surprise greater than the question of why it didn't happen sooner.

(*gestures her hands in the air to signify a headline*)

Eleanor Winifred Stanton, dies by own hand of an overdose of Demerol and Jack Daniels. Stay true to American tradition, I always say. And if I'm to go, I want to go out with a helluva buzz, because the bang lost its kick way too long ago.

(*She makes her way over to to a makeup table*)

That my final farewell shall be broadcast live over national television is an even more fitting irony. But the sleeping masses must be jolted from their catatonic states, their blind devotion to mediocrity. When my broadcast goes out over live television, Wimbley and his secret service will not be able to silence the truth any further. A truth which begs to be heard. All Wimbely's spin doctors and all his media puppets will be forced to watch reality as it happens to them, and in the twenty minutes or so it will take for them to find me, my swan song will be the new national anthem.

(She sits down at her makeup table, pours another strong drink into the chrystal goblet from the open bottle of Jack Daniels, and takes her seat before the mirror. She gazes into the mirror a few moments, appalled at what she sees. She talks as she stares at her own face in the mirror.)

How have I come to this place, weary and broken and in the depths of despair after living a life of regal purpose? For a lack of a politer term, I began the long descent into darkness the night "Wimpy" Foster Stanton "retired" me. Turned me in for a younger model, one whose..."skin"... was tighter and whose beautiful face might not remind him of his own mortality. In the process of natural selection she became the screaming participant of his sperm donations. In that sense, this new aff`air reflected a law of the jungle that is not so new after all.

(goes to table for drink sees a famed picture of them in a happier time)

There was once a time when reality was so clear. The hours of a day were sanctioned, entries in an appointment book. How we would fly from one appointment to the other - 'good morning misses president. It is an honor mister president. Welcome to our country mister and misses president.' We had purpose, Foster and I. The moments in an hour precious, and we seemed on the brink of some great discovery. The country was there, behind us, propelling us forward on this great cloud of change. Before the poison wind blew across the land and turned us into spirits of destruction.

(sits down with picture at makeup table)

It begins at an ending. When I discovered the man I loved in the arms of a woman young enough to be his daughter. In that second I realized that the only law is Darwin's Law, the survival of the youngest and the tittiest.

In the judgement of the man I had devoted my life to, it was time for an oil change.

(She takes a framed photograph of him, shatters it on the edge of the makeup table. She removes the photo from the broken glass.)

Well "Wimpy", I shall not go quietly into that good night. I will go scratching and clawing and screaming and hanging on for dear life, for liberty, and all of this in the face of death.

(She uses a pair of scissors and cuts the photograph into little peices)

Your likeness is but a false front, a movie set held up with shints and wire. What I found inside the man was a vicious monster, nothing like the innocence I knew when we were young. Before the __sickness... enveloped him in its shroud.

(slowly brushes the pieces off the table and watches them fall to the floor. Turns to herself in the mirror)

I used to be so young and pretty. I even made prom queen in high school. All the boys wanted me. All those young men of rich New England families. Their own breeding was their stock in trade. They reeked of race horses, old money and Kennedy whiskey. Men of class? Let's get real. They all wanted to screw me.

Well I wanted to screw them! Because you see, in the absence of real love, one reaches for the substitute. But if I didn't feel some semblance of love, as I did with Foster...Ah, sex, that sweet sacharine of youth!

(She opens the plastic prescription pill bottle, and pours a handful of pills out into her hand. She deliberates on them, then pops them all at once, washing them down with the Jack Daniels, then addresses herself in the mirror again.)

Well that is fine, and perhaps fitting the world should see me as I really am. Without the makeup, without the lights that hide the imperfections of age. Without the lights that hide the imperfections of age. Without the image builders who mold public opinion and the media who follow them in sheep-like obedience.

(Gets up grabs the bottle, takes a long swig and puts it on the small oval table next to the padded chair. She takes a deep breath.)

My awareness of Truth. How did that begin? It was the dream. Walking in the darkness down Pennsylvania Avenue and I spotted the White House, majestic in its stone silence. It looked like a giant white ghost thrust through manicured lawns grown thick with blood and money.

Something struck me odd this night, it's walls turned from brilliant white to sheer glass, and I could see the rooms and hallways inside, brightly lit by lamp fixtures. Gone from an angelic white to a crimson red. Like a giant dolls house. I saw tiny figures going through their motions, unaware they were being observed by this shadow in the darkness, small in her insignificance

Spirits of the past were in the air, visions of romance and southern states, bribery and passion, in that glass house I saw suffering and pain and love and a yearning for a higher power that was not God. In that dream, I knew their hidden secrets, their buried lies. I had gazed into the glass house as all the others had gazed upon what I felt werethe privacies of my own life. I saw then there were no secrets, not in this dream, and not in the real world. Then I awoke in the Oval Bedroom, Foster snoring by my side, and I remember then how much I loved him.

(She opens an old shoebox filled with torn envelopes and letters)

I still have all of his letters. I called him Johnny. He called me Trixie, cause he said I had this trick of changing my look, my expressions, so that I appeared to be a different person.

(She opens a letter and begins to read)

'My dearest Trixie, My undying love for you is like an eternal flame that burns relentlessly in my universe, a fire that shall never be quenched but in the comfort of your embrace. We shall together become one in our pursuit of the dream. Our dream of being together forever. We will change the world together. Love Johnny.'

We were so in love!

(reflective)

Wimbley Foster Stanton had chosen me as his lawfully wedded wife. I first saw him when I was in the tenth grade. I thought he was gallant, even with his lisp. He was captain of the football team, even then a winner. He waited a month before screwing me, right there on the high school soccer field, on a beautiful June night where I would like to say I lost my virginity but that was already a road well travelled.

When he finally did, I remember I felt something stir within my heart for the first time in my life.

(this brings on great sadness)
Ah yes.

(long pause)

Love.

(the memories flooding back)

There was happiness in the early years. Weekends in Cape Cod, the summers on his sailboat. The sun and salt against our tan, brown skin. Dreams of affecting change in the legislature always in the air, circling like sea gulls above our heads, ambition and drive and desire in that heady mix of sex and greed disguised as idealism.

We'd drink in the bars along the shore, dancing and talking and laughing. Our old friends told us even then we'd probably one day give the democrats a run for their money when we reached Washington. But for then we still had our innocence. It hung in the air like the warm glow of neon beer signs and the sweet smell of cooked crab and corn, the genuine laughter of kids on their way to war. Soldiers on their way to the battleground of politics.

(laughing)

Welcome to the glass house. They check in but they don't check out. Well we checked in. Wimbley Foster Stanton entered into office, and it was he who ran the Vietnam War. He bombed 'em to hell and back, gave Hanoi a run they will never forget. That was when I began my real tenure as the First Lady. That was when my indentured servitude really began.

Many was the night I spent on my back for my husband, earning him his contributions the old fashioned way. There were oil men, sheiks, shysters, bankers and lawyers. Men who smelled of ancient colognes and laundered money. Men who pushed buttons and bought favors. All those spectres who would come to haunt him like poltergeists in a southern mansion.

The day we entered the Oval Office, we stepped out of the limousine outside of the gates, and it was all a show. The flashbulbs going off, with reporters in their JC Penney suits. 'Misses President, how will you decorate the white house?' I should have told them by the blood of soldiers and Christ and all them be damned!

(observes with reverence the photographs on the walls)

I remember how we stood on that fine lawn and watched those majestic walls and that flag. Like something out of National

Geographic. Vietnam was on my mind constantly, and I began to speak out against the war effort to my closest friends. When Wimpy heard about this, as he heards about anything I said or thought, he showed me a side of the mask I never wanted to see.

He told me "do not wander back into Cambodia, my dearest Eleanor. You could yourself caught in a land mine that could blast you straight to hell." Now THAT was the order of the day and the ultimate truth, for I didn't know my husband's contribution to the war was not an honorable one, but one that was politically expediant.

(LONG PAUSE, great grief, anger and pain)

That horrid war and those bombs in their searing fury, that was the way my heart went up the day he told me I was finished. The day he told me she would take my place in his heart and in his bed. This child who could be his daughter, the one who now possessed the tools for the desirable evolution of his species. Then would come the inevitible heartbreak and despair, and the fallout from such a discovery.

I thought of the other First Ladies before me. How would I cope with such bitter dsappointment? No tea and sympathy for Eleanor, no women's club luncheons or

Rotary club speeches about how it was being the wife of the President of the United States.

Talking about the things that were and the things that should have been. Not for this old girl. Because that is all just hypothetical naval gazing bullshit. He would not divorce me, even his press secretary agreed that it would make for bad press. so we kept up the illusion of the dance. I would live in the White House with him, yet have no part in his life. He moved her to an apartment within walking distance of the oval office, a walk he would never have to make in the air conditioned comfort of the presidential limousine.

Or he would summon her when he thought I was asleep. But my light was always on. I never slept a moment in the White House. And I've become weary from the pain, and long for that sweet delicious sleep that only death can bring. My shrink told me, 'Trixie, it's just something he's going through.' Yeah. No shit.

The great Mid-Life Crisis, the Male Menopause. That never ending cycle of life-dance in which man always seems to emerge the triumphant victor. For those rich with money and power, such as Wimbley Foster

Stanton, there will never be a shortage of young willing flesh. A perfect metaphor for politics. A perfect breeding ground for the mid-life crisis, the purchase of new skin for the old ceremony. What in the end, is the final thought or conclusion of the life of Eleanor Winifred Stanton? That she was born and bred to serve the ends of men whose ambition would override their sense of humanity?

Or perhaps to service the insatiable need of animals in pursuit of the ultimate breeder? I believe my life was a monument to a life of servitude, but in the end a tombstone to strength.

To go out a coward, some would say, at the mercy of some God in the face of self-administered medications? It is a fitting tribute to strength and courage, for it takes a will of steel to not only endure the brutality of politics, but to face the demons of the unknown darkness completely alone. For all those "strong" men, in their vicious struggle to overcome their opponants and to accumulate as much wealth as possible, all fear what I dare to face.

The ultimate darkness. The great beyond, that mystery that lies behind the curtain. They run from it like cowering dogs in their whipped submissions. When you watch them strutting like roosters on the floor of the senate, don't be fooled by their false bravado. No. They are hanging on to their survival instincts, white knuckling it, hanging from the cliffs by their manicured fingernails as the waves crash at the dark rocks below.

(she picks up the phone, dials)

Hello Robert. I'm ready. Remember, not a word to them where I am when they call. Tell them I ordered you to do this. I'm ready. And Robert? Thank you for setting this up for me.

(pause)

I can't tell you that, Robert. It's okay. I'm fine.

(She takes a long drink)

Here goes nothing, old girl.

(She turns the camera on, steps back and looks into the lens. She straightens herself, and suddenly, seemingly sober, becomes regal once again.)

This is my final farewell to you, my public. An invisible audience of spectators who never knew what went on behind the castle walls. Before my departure tonight, you will know what happened inside the glass house. How I became an indentured servant to the intoxicating power of the oval office, and hence, became a casualty of war. I have been your first lady during the reign of the great King, President elect Wimbley Foster Stanton. In my servitude to him I have done you a great disservice.

I have been the accomplice in the creation of an illusion of security and false hope. I stand before you tonight as a messenger of truth, and hope you will not see me as a martyr, but as a bearer of the light. I am here to tell you that the way to freedom is not through blind obediance, but in the seeking of real truth. You will not find it in the evening news, or written in the press releases of what you believe to be democracy. You will find it within your hearts, and within your inner voices, and I pray you will not have to find it the way I did.

What I learned during my brief tenure in the glass house was that if you think you have freedom in a land of the free, you are mistaken. Because all the while you shout for it, it is being taken from you, one right at a time. When at last you realize it is missing, it will be too late. These years of servitude to you were not as they seemed.

To those who would envy us for our stature, for our portension of power, you could not see what lay on the inside of our hearts. You could not see the erosion that ate away at our psyches by each passing second of the clock. You could also not know that while you were sleeping a government operates independently of the democratic process. It was formed to circumvent the congress of this great land, and it has survived by the order of the president and all of his men.

While you are sleeping in your warm houses, they are out there, planning takeovers of communist governments and organizing complex assassinations, setting up puppet regimes and padding their pockets with the sale of weapons and drugs.

I am here to tell you that the delegates you have elected have fooled you into thinking you had some control over their appointments. But as your first lady, I must say to you that what you have heard in the media is only the tip of the iceberg. Because although you think you can see inside the transparent walls of the glass house, you do not see any semblance of real truth.

Your president and his secret service and all of his image contractors have sold you a bill of goods, and I can tell you they have eroded our constitution into a useless pile of dust. They were not the first to do this, and if you do not hear what I have to say to you tonight, they will not be the last. All of my misgivings and all of my actions cannot mean a thing unless I can inspire you to action.

The men who came before you were willing to give their lives to the cause of freedom. What are you willing to give? And do you have the courage and the fortitude to effect positive change? Will you cast out those who would corrupt all that has gone toward the building of the American dream? I am imploring of you that your actions from this point on will determine how much longer this charade will be played. I leave in my wake a two hundred page document naming names of those within your government responsible for the mess it has become. Wimbley Foster Stanton heads the list.

But there is an even greater injustice that has been done here, and that is an injustice of the Spirit. That your president would put his dick before his people is nothing new, but that he would lie to you and to me in the name of democracy is the real tragedy. For that there is no forgiveness.

For years I played my role with the civility and dignity of a devoted patron saint. But all the while the charade was played it sank deeper and deeper into the mire, and I became a person trapped inside the role of an actor who doesn't believe in their character anymore. I had ignored what my conscience told me was not the right thing to do, and I sit before you now and confess to you I was wrong.

I recognize the deception for what it is, and cannot allow it to go on any longer. My question to you, the American public, is how much longer will you allow it to go on? That being said, what have I learned from this harsh reality? That I had no control over your president, or anyone else on this earth. God knows I tried to hang onto the past because it was a known thing and didn't make me afraid to face it. From that painful reality I have heard the voice of my own inner heart. It is a voice that has spoken silently to me since I can remember, but it is only now I have chose to listen.

The voice has said: 'If there be a white light that shines out across the sands of time brilliant in its opalescence, then the shadow figure which emerges from it is not merely an insignificant speck on the horizon. We are but columns of light, made of the same light that makes up the shine of stars and the particles of atoms.'

But to those who have stayed close to Source, the brightness is pure, and the light is energy, and it is love and it is Eternal. Man forgets that in his selfish duality."

Well, they all forget that in Washington.

Now, as I reach my life's end, where could I go after a lifetime of servitude in the ranks of deception and the living of someone elses' dream? A dream impure of heart and purpose and devoid of all humanity? Straight to hell in a handbasket, as Harry Truman once said.

(she hears something)

I can hear them approaching from downstairs, now. they know I am here. His secret service men will come crashing through the door, their revolvers drawn, to discover me dead.

(She picks up the gun. we hear running footsteps, frantic voices of men approaching the door.)

Well, my grateful public, let it be said that Eleanor Winifred Stanton was not afraid to go over that precipace into the eternal darkness. That is the ultimate act of courage. To those that will follow me into the glass house, and finally into the abyss that is eternity, my final farewell to them be this: Walk into the light always, and follow your heart. No matter how much you compromise your being know that in the end, you will only have the final truth to answer to. Choose carefully those who will lead you into servitude, and remember always that in a democracy, it is the people who must rule, not those who have been elected.

Walk in Life as I do in the face of my death, with truth, with courage, and with the knowledge that in the final accounting, no one escapes the terrible, sweet sleep that will be my epitaph.

VOICES: Misses President! Misses President! Open the door Misses President! We want to help you!

(frantic pounding on the door; men's voices rising, ready to break down the door. Eleanor

raises the gun and places it to her temple,
looking upward to the heavens in supplication,
a classic martyr stance.

BLACKOUT - CURTAIN

Voodoo Moon

SETTING: *A police interrogation room.*

CHARACTER: *A middle aged black woman named MAYA WATSON is standing at center stage. She is dressed in shabby clothing. She wears a colorful scarf around her head/ Haiti-style. Maya is a very wise woman, street smart and intelligent beyond her years. She has seen the dark side of life and has lived to tell about it. But she is still a woman born from poverty and a limited formal education. The room is stark but for a metal chair and perhaps a metal conference table. The chair sits in a pale circle of light. She is illuminated by the spotlight. There is a two way mirror in the room, behind which she addresses her invisible spectators.*

MAYA

So you men with your analytical minds believe you can get to the heart of the matter, to make sense of how the spirit world can manifest effective change in a cold and seemingly uncaring universe?

(laughing)

You will try. But your Western minds will not be able to see past the wall of illusion science has constructed around itself. To reach across the abyss of understanding and build a bridge across to the other side. I don't think that's something you are prepared to do. If you are looking for a confession of guilt, of wrongdoing, you will not get it, not the way you think. Because I did what I had to do. I had to rid the world of one small source of pain and suffering. Did I kill Lawrence Tyrone Watson? That's what you really want to know, isn't it? The lawyers and the district attorney and the police, not to mention the psychologists and criminologists all trying to make sense of what happened to him?

(laughing)

Why, you read the medical reports, right? The man died in he's sleep, plain and simple. He must've had a bad dream, by the look in he's eyes I'd swear the man saw a goddamn ghost. Couldn't wipe that look off his face for nothing. They buried the man looking like he'd been haunted to the grave. For gods sake he looked like he was so scared he shit himself ten times over, was frozen stiff like an old black popsicle.

The man was ugly enough in life but Christ almighty did he look bad when he cacked! Not that the undertaker had much to work with, mind you. Old Doc Dixon said he looked like a zombie, like he'd gone out with the curse of the devil on him, uh huh.

(laughs)

Well maybe there was some truth to that after all. Not that he didn't deserve to go out of this life like that. I mean, the man dealt with death, that was his life. Honeyboy Watson was known from uptown to the projects. Uh-huh. Sold his rock to any kid, housewife or teenager who gave him the dollar to do it. he didn't have no qualms about that. Honeyboy was a equal opportunity dealer, yeah he was.

(she grows angry)

And I was a terrorized wife living in the projects. Another victim of circumstance, a statistic for the social workers and another newspaper story. An obiturary just waiting to happen. Not that any of you could have prevented it.

(happy, remembering a more innocent time)

I married Honeyboy when we was only sixteen. We wasn't drinking then, we wasn't doing drugs. It was nineteen sixty seven. Martha and the Vandellas playing Heat Wave out of Chicago. Motown was hot, and got our kicks going to the parties all along Harvey Street. We lost a lot of friends in Vietnam, but we was in a different world. We were so in love, yeah we were. We'd go to Wrigley Park and watch the kids shooting hoops, not drugs.

It was Summer In The City, with James Brown playing at the High Five and Chuck

Berry was live at Flory Auditorium. We didn't
see the needles and we didn't notice the blow,
but it had crept into our lives just the same. It
had taken the families and divided them, had
taken fathers from their children and made
widows of too many young mothers. Like a
black hawk it had swept down on us and
preyed on our children.

While Motown played on the airwaves across
the hot Chicago night, Honeyboy and me, we
found our own Shangra-La, walking along
shoreline drive and imagining we'd someday
get a nice house and join the swells who lived
and partied along the waterfront.

Honeyboy and me, we sang gospel in the
choir at Brighton Baptist Congregation and I
remember how proud his mama was when
she saw us all dressed in our white
robes. She said she always knew he'd sing
praises to the lord, and she was proud of me,
too. She treated me like a daughter, mama
did, uh huh.

She came to the church every Sunday and she
watched him sing and one day afte the service
we were having pot luck at the church hall
and she said she couldn't stop watching
Honeyboy cause he looked so handsome in
his gown, and she could pretend he had
graduated high school when she saw him
dressed like that. But she laughed cause he
was so black and his head poking up out the
white gown, she said he looked like a raisin

in the sun, and that weas probably account of his father, uh huh. But see, that was long ago.

The times changed, and with it a radical shift to darkness. We had our kids, and we all watched as Honeyboy became a part of the street and the shadows of the projects. With all our high flying dreams of youth, we didn't realize then we'd never make it out of the Robert Taylor projects.

So the Jekyll and Hyde transformation of Lawrence Honeyboy Watson had begun, and he went from being the saint of Simon Street to the anti-Christ himself.

I would like to say it was the drugs and the alcohol that did him in. But I believe now it was the loa, a dark spirit of the old world congo that overtook him, and he was defenseless to fight it.

My grandmother came from a long line of slaves brought to New Orleans from Africa, and she was a woman who knew about such things. She was one of the old practitioners of 'Houdoo,' and had helped bring it to the United States. She knew Madam Laveau, and had met Papa Doc John, and had learned everything she knew directly from the source.

She had known the immense power of the gods, of the loa, the ancient spirits of voodoo, and she had the power of second sight to know how to apply it and what its final outcome would be. She passed this power on to her bloodline, my mother, my sisters and I. But we never knew it.

All I ever knew were the dreams, the nightmares, the premonitions of death and destruction. But she always told me I had the gift.

And as the shadow of death crept into our hearts and into our streets, it became an omen. The nightmares increased. Our people were dying. The bad loa had taken over our youth and turned our cities into a den of urban terror. I knew something had to be done.

But what could I do? A welfare mother married to a crack-addicted drug-dealing drunk? So I climbed those rickety stairs to the roof of that God forsaken tenement.

(sings)

'Up the ladder to the roof - where we can see Heaven much better.'

(laughing)

And I stood at the edge of that building, looking far, far below.

(looking down to an imaginary drop)

There was a cool wind kicking up from across Lake Michigan and I felt like almighty God as I stood on the roof of Robert Taylor Projects looking down at the dirty street and wondering what it would be like to fly. The place stunk, even in the breeze, it smelted like somebody had died and rotted beneath the floorboards. It was the smell of death, cheap booze and whores with old perfume. It was the smell of crack and old bones, of fires long gone dead.

Then I looked down again, measuring the long drop to the street. There were small black figures down there, shoeless joes all of them, living in the depths of despair and poverty. Most of them would end up dead or in jail. There was no way but up, and a voice spoke to me from the dark, from an ancient land and place.

It was the voice of my grandmother calling back to me, and her message was clear. "You shall go forth among them and give them strength."

"You shall unleash the power of the mojo, of the loa, and summon to your command all the spirits of the universe to quell the disease that has spread across this land."

And it was an old, ancient power, you see. Something that had been born in the deepest jungles of the dark continent. It had been conjured from the most primitive men from the caves and trees and from around fires. It was summoned from ancient evenings from the dust of idols long ago forgotten, and man's great deities were carved from wood, not imagined from glittering temples and biblical verse. And there it travelled in the great ships across the Atlantic passage, inside the men and women and children who had been chained and held captive.

Do you want to to know why this power had travelled with the slaves to the new world? It was justice. A different kind of justice that you behind that glass would not understand. An eye for an eye, congo style, uh-huh.

In those days the captives dared not speak of their gods, their idols, and their masters forbade them to speak of the voodoo. They saw it as a threat to their great Christ, whom they had created in their own image. They were afraid of the power that it had. It scared the living hell out of them.

But the captives spoke of it just the same, and used dolls and secret codes to practice their magic until it became so powerful that it could no longer be ignored. It was happening in Haiti, and the slaves stateside could feel it, even from the highest of plantation walls.

Then came that long and terrible night of fire, the night Haiti was taken by the captives. It was a night those who had feared the natives had hoped would never come. To this day most of Haiti believes in voodoo, and it exists behind every shadow in New Orleans.

And it is alive and well in the back alleys and the tenements of Chicago. I know. Because I put it there. So you want to know how I killed Honeyboy Watson? I killed him but I never touched him. I killed him with the power of the voodoo. I danced and I sang and I allowed the loa to enter me, and it was then I felt the spirit of my deceased grandmother enter me, empowering me with her spirit.

I could feel the power coursing through me, like electric wires on fire with the prana of the ages. I became acutely aware of the oneness I had with all things living. I saw the dark ones that lived inside of my husband, and I knew they could never be removed. He yelled at the top of his diseased lungs, 'Where is my dinner, woman?' as he realized the chicken I had bought was not in the oven or on his dinner plate. It sat raw and uncooked at the center of an altar I had placed in our bedroom, flanked by candles and fruit. It was my offering to the spirits.

But a larger sacrifice was needed, uh-huh. I realized that Honeyboy was the only person on this earth that would do. He stood there, high and laughing as he grabbed my hair and smacked me across the face with his fist. But I felt no pain, and there was no blood. He could not believe this, so he hit me again, harder. And again, even harder. I could feel

the spirits rising within me, the power
building.

    'To all those whose names are
    remembered To all those whose names
    are forgotten I give you bo eat
    To all those who have come before
    To all those who will come after
    I offer sustenance!'

And he screamed at me! 'What are these red
candles, bitch, these bowls filled with food
and drink, incense and dirt?' And I told him!
You stupid ass! They are the sacraments for
the ritual 1 Rada! Dahomie! Azaka! Hear my
calling to you, o great powers of the Congo!

Legba! Arzulie! Masa! He is waiting for you,
your sacrifice awaits you! Honeyboy's eyes is
sticking out their sockets like big ole grapes!

'You have gone mad, woman!' he yelled, and
hit me again, but I pushed him away, could
see in his eyes the fear of the afflicted. The
look of an animal that knows it's going to die.
He swung at me, but I pushed him away
again. 'Yaguo! Yameya! I beseech of you!
Take this man for your power, take him from
this life, take him away from the living so he
can do no more harm!'

I could see his face, this strange look, like
somone who just realizes they've been
poisoned. He clutched at his throat, he began
to choke. It was my first impulse to help him.

But how could I help this man who had tried to kill me so many times before? This man who had brought so much misery to so many others? And I was after all, killing him. No, there would be no help for Honeyboy Watson, a man who would leave no legacy. Only an epitaph of pain and suffering. I watched him clutch at his throat, his lungs, his heart. He fell at my feet, gasping for breath. I did not dare move a muscle, but felt the winds like a tempest inside of me, a hurricane of psychic energies swirling in a cosmic cloud.

I saw terrible visions of suffering spirits, fires from distant days, and the explosion of stars blowing outward in specks of orange cosmic dust hurlting through space. A nova had ignited, somewhere, in some galaxy I could not explain, and then, as quickly as it had burst, it was dark again.

(she becomes very quiet, as if living the experience. She looks down)

Lawrence Honeyboy Watson was dead, laying at my feet. For once, he was quiet, and I remember how strange it seemed seeing him so motionless and without hate. A calm had come over me, and the spirits had gone, flown from my being as angels cascading into the heavens and the orisha had disappeared to their own corner of the universe.

Whatever demons had been there, whatever terrible spirits had witnessed the destruction or taken part in it, had descended into hell, down a dark furnace. Into the night. I walked to the window. It was night and crystal clear, I could see a full moon glaring down in all its brilliance. I remember thinking that it looked like... a voodoo moon. Culled from ancient evenings and borne from the smoke of a distant fire. I placed a jacket on my shoulders and walked to the liquor store
and dialed nine-one-one.

(she dials an imaginary payphone)

'Yes, my name is Maya Watson. I would like to report a homicide. I live at nine six nine Gideon Street, Apartment two four five in the Robert Taylor Projects. Please send an ambulance.'

(pause)

Yes I will be there to meet the police. Thank you, good-night.'

(pauses for effect)

I walked home that night for the first time I had no fear. I was not worried about anything. For I knew in my heart that there would be no more pain and suffering, at least where Honeyboy was concerned. As I sauntered home beneath that....voodoo moon, past the drug dealers and the thieves, the rapists and the murderers, a new golden age was dawning, uh-huh.

I remembered the words of my grandmother. I was the chosen one for which this god-forsaken place had been waiting for so long. If the police and the social workers and the justice system and the prisons couldn't rid this place of the vermin that had overrun it, then I, armed with the power of the loa, with the spirit of the Orisha, I could make a difference. And that is exactly what I did.

And instead of hiding in their apartments, I could see my friends as they walked along the street, their fear was gone!

(waves her arm, recognizing someone)

'Hello Misses Hilliard. How is Duncan, did he ever get that night shift back again? He did? God bless him, and let him know I was asking about him.' 'Oh Mildred Watkins! I haven't seen you in ages. I trust you'll be in church this Sunday. I'll see you there. And make sure you bring your lovely daughter Tomika. In a few years she'll be turning all the boys heads.'

(turns her attention back to the two way mirror)

Effective change, gentlemen, for which not a single tax dollar was spent, except to cart the bodies away. And have your detectives and police noticed that the neighborhood around Robert Taylor just hasn't been the same these days? Them dealers seem to be droppping like flies, dying off in the strangest of manners, uh-huh.

(laughing)

Reverend Samuels say he don't know if its a blessin or a curse, but it's a shame so many of our young people are dying like they are. But what is really strange is how the good ones that had gone astray are scared straight nowadays, cause they notice its only the bad ones that don't learn that are dying.

(laughing)

Well gentlemen, that is my story. And I know you have no evidence to hold me here, now do ya?

(she waits. From the speaker there emerges a resigned male voice)

VOICE
No Misses Watson. We don't. You are free to go.

MAYA
Why thank you, gentlemen. And if any of you happen to be down around Gideon Street, do drop by, uh-huh. Cause the neighborhood ain't like it used to be. We got a lot of folk

down there who will be glad to welcome you into their hearts and into their homes. But if it's just the same to you, don't mention what we've talked about here today. It wouldn't be fittin, nor proper. And if it's a full moon night, the kinda moon that don't look right, keep on going.

It means we're working late.

LIGHTS DOWN.

CURTAIN.

Introduction to The Waiting Room

This was one of the first plays I both produced and directed at a number of Los Angeles area theaters. It is a One-Act centering around a couple trapped in a limbo between purgatory and Heaven. Although it is a great piece for two actors, some of the individual speeches can stand alone as monologues.

Waiting Room

"Waiting Room" centers around a man and a woman who havejust committed suicide and are trapped in a limbo statebetween the physical world and the hereafter. The room contains only a table, two chairs a 38 caliber revolver, anda booklet explaining The Rules.

The couple is forced to play a game by a controlling demi-God named The Warden, who remains an invisibleomnipresence. This Russian Roulette game is played byconfession and catharsis, dictating that the players reveal a secret about their lives before spinning the barrel, placing the gun to temple, and pulling the trigger. The player who "dies" by the gun has been promised passage to Heaven, while the other must stay behind to play the Game forever.

The Game gives these two opposing characters a chance atredemption and change, while exploring with dark humor our concepts of God, Heaven, Sin and The Value of Life. It is the playwright's intent to show that suicide isn't worthcomitting, can cause dire consequences to those loved onesleft behind, and that life, although sometimes cruel andunfair, is worth living if you can figure out the trick todealing with its pain in order to experience the joy.

CHARACTERS:

KAYE LEAVENTHAL ... Mid 30's, a real estate woman from Los Angeles. Slightly manic, neurotic. Attracive in a conservative way.

ADRIAN TOPITSKY... 30-40's, a polish Jew from Philadelphia, a bearded intelectual . Wire frame glasses.

SETTING:
Bare stage, preferably a black cyclorama. There is adoorway, behind which is placed a bare white stage light, as large and bright as possible. If a corridor can be fashionedfrom either wood or black cloth, so much the better. In the center of the stage sits a plain wooden table, which can also be a pane of glass set on a pedestal. On this table sits a booklet and a 38 calibre revolver. There are two chairs facing one another on either side of the table.

A tiffany or hooded lamp can be hung over the table, illuminating the table itself. If budget allows, a fog machine using dry ice concealed offstage can add to theeerie, dreamlike effect the play conveys. Mood lighting,dark and subdued, is suggested, as well as the selectionof "SPACE" or "NEW AGE" music for pro-curtain, and postcurtain. We recommend music from "Enya's" "WATERMARK" cd, playing prior to curtain leading up to "Evening Falls,"followed by "Cursum Perficio" during curtain and while Kayewalks out of the Light. This completes the mood to a dramatic degree and should not be overlooked by the stagemanager.

PROPS:
.38 Caliber revolver, Booklet, Bullet.

MUSIC/SOUND CUES:
Kaye's suicide note on tape, repeating industrial soundingbuzzer, gun barrel clicking, gun firing, sound of industrialnoise, such as steam and compression escaping, machineryclanking, techno noise/industrial, steam locomotive.

WAITING ROOM
(Prior to curtain, pump smoke onto surface of stage, withspecial emphasis on the corridor area. Intensify the lightbeneath the curtain, raising the music to "CURSUM PERFICIO"By Enya. HOUSE LIGHTS DOWN.)

CURTAIN OPENS

(KAYE LEAVENTHAL stands at the end of the corridor in a long white nightgown, {or in the doorway if there is no corridor} She is backlit by the light in such a way as to give her anangelic ethereal look. As she stands motionless in the light, we HEAR her voice, preferably from a tape source, orit can be done live. Music is still playing.)

KAYE'S VOICE (voiceover)
'To Whom It May Concern: I am leaving this note as my final farewell to this life, an existence that has been fraught with pain, disallusionment, loneliness, and anger. I have decided there is no point in suffering any longer. The loss of my daughter, Michelle, and the slow agonizing death of a loveless marriage has brought me to purgatories edge. I do not believe there is a God, but if there is one, may he look upon my soul with compassion. If there be an existence in the hereafter, allow my soul to be in the kingdom of Heaven. I love you with all my heart, signed, Kaye Leaventhal.'

SOUND FX of steam and industrial type noises and a BUZZER SOUNDING as Kaye walks slowly from the blinding whiteness of the light down the corridor. A flashing red light bulbblinks above the doorway. LIGHT UP on ADRIAN TOPTISKY, seated

motionless at the table, his hands folded.
SOUND FX DOWN as Kaye approaches the
table.

> ADRIAN
> Come in. Relax. Although that may
> be quite difficult, considering the
> circumstances.

> KAYE
> What is this? Where am I?

> ADRIAN
> The question isn't where you are.
> It's where you're going.

> KAYE
> Is this some kind of joke?

> ADRIAN
> You could say that. But if that's
> the case, then the joke would be on
> both of us.

*Kaye looks around in disbelief. THE DOOR
SLAMS SHUT behind her. (Fishing line rigged
to a pulley and the doorknob works nicely) She
walks slowly into the room, examining the
strange scenery around her. Adrian studies her
closely.*

> ADRIAN
> Have a seat. Relax. The memory will
> start to come back.

KAYE
I demand to know where we are.
Are you some kind of freak?

ADRIAN
What was the last thing you
remember?

(She strains to remember)

KAYE
I was home. I'd taken sleeping
pills. A lot of them. Then there
was a long corridor... a blinding
white light.

ADRIAN
Anything else?

KAYE
There were sounds, voices. They
sounded like... angels. Singing out
of tune.

ADRIAN
The Warden really needs to hire
himself some new singers.

*She spreads her hands in front of her, trying to
make sure she's really there.*

KAYE
Am I dead or alive?

ADRIAN
Technically, we're both dead. But
then, we'd stopped really living a
long time ago.

KAYE
What is this place? And who the
hell are you?

*Adrian gets up from the table and extends his
hand to her. She doesn't take it.*

ADRIAN
Allow me to introduce myself. I'm
Adrian Toptisky. Writer. Teacher.
God's gift to women. And this....is
the waiting room.

KAYE
Are you sure you're not Rod
Serling?

ADRIAN
This is serious. It's time for
retribution. Time to do your
penance to the Warden.

KAYE
Warden?

ADRIAN
Yeah. He runs the place. He's got a
helluva voice. I think he used to
be in radio.

Kaye makes a mad dash for the door. She pulls on it and bangs on it, but it won't open. She bangs on the darkness of the empty backdrops, but her fists won't make contact.

KAYE
Let me out of here!

ADRIAN
Go ahead and try if it makes you feel better. I gave up after the first week.

KAYE
(turning on him)
You don't have any right to keep me here against my will.

ADRIAN
It's not my choice to make. It's the Warden's. I'm just a player. Players don't make the rules.

KAYE
(frustrated)
Oh Christ. I don't believe this.

ADRIAN
Just relax and enjoy it. I'm not such a bad guy, once you get to know me.

(excited)

Hey, wanna know how I killed
myself? I took a skydive off the
top of the World Trade Center
Building in downtown Manhattan.
One Hundred ten stories to the
street, sister, and they go by fast
without a parachute. You wanna
talk about a mess?

It was a Rembrant, right there on
the sidewalk. Man, the people were
so fascinated.

A vendor came by and started
selling popcorn and hot dogs till
the police got there. I even made
the six o clock news!

KAYE
I don't want to hear about this. I
don't care about your life or how
you got here or anything else.
I just want to know how I can get
out of here.

ADRIAN
Oh, you're a real sweetheart. You
know, I was married to a woman like
you. Her name was Ellen. She was
neurotic. And a manic-depressive.
And if you don't mind my saying so,
she was also a bitch.

KAYE

Uh...EXCUSE ME??? Did you just call
me what I thought you did?

ADRIAN

Let me explain something to
you...what is your name?

KAYE
    (sternly)
Kaye Leaventhal.

ADRIAN

Yeah. Kaye. See, in the material
world, we avoid direct
confrontations. We're afraid of
stepping out of our boundaries.
Problem is, we stay locked inside
our self-imposed prisons and never
connect with anyone. That's how we
die, only to discover after we die
that it could have been better.
Here in the Waiting Room, we speak
truths. We don't mince words. Which
brings me right back to the fact
you are a bitch.

KAYE

I am not going to sit by and take
this kind of abuse. I demand you
release me from this place at once!

ADRIAN
Believe me, you should be in no
hurry. Here, time has no meaning.
There are no clocks. Only the
tedious passing of the endless
contiuum.

KAYE
Wonderful.

He pulls out a chair for her. She pulls
it away from him and places it where
she wants it. He paces around the
table.

ADRIAN
Before my--accident, I thought
when you pulled the plug on
yourself, you either went to meet
your maker. Or there was nothing
but blackness.

Poof! Eternal nothingness. A dark
hole in the void. And from that
nothingness would come peace, a
respite from the madness of
existence. An oasis from the
lonliness that had engulfed me.

KAYE
I'm touched.

ADRIAN
I ended up here, just like you.

                    KAYE
And where is here?

                    ADRIAN
Here is nowhere. And this nowhere
replaced the nothingness that I
thought would be here if here
wasn't really here.

                    KAYE
I have no idea what you're talking
about.

                    ADRIAN
You will.

                    KAYE
   (staring at pistol)
Why is there a gun sitting on this
table?

*Adrian picks up the booklet and hands it to
her.*

                    ADRIAN
This says it better than I ever
could. Written by the Warden
himself.

Kaye reads from the booklet.

                    KAYE
 'Instruction Guide For The Waiting
Room, A Dead Man's Guide To A
Happier Afterlife. By The Warden.'

ADRIAN
Smug bastard, isn't he?

KAYE
I notice it says 'A Dead MAN'S
guide.'

ADRIAN
You're not one of those liberated
feminisms are you?

KAYE
I take it you don't believe in
equality for women?

ADRIAN
Oh Jesus. We're DEAD here, Kaye.

KAYE
...and obviously this Warden
doesn't either.

ADRIAN
It doesn't mean that. Just read the
damn thing.

KAYE
You know the more I listen to you
the less I like you.

ADRIAN
(*irritated*)
We are stuck in a time cube
somewhere out in Einstein's worst
nightmare. We may possibly be
stuck here for eternity. Can we go
on?

*She stares at him for a long second, a look of
contempt and seething hatred. She's about to
sound off on him, but holds her tongue. She
reluctantly continues reading.*

KAYE
'Welcome to the Waiting Room,
the passage between the material
world and the forever after. Since
you have chosen death by your own
hand, you will determine by
confession and chance the outcome
of your future.

You are not spirits, but flesh and
blood persons, given back your
original bodies for this test.
Should you decide to not cooperate
in the Game, you will be consigned
to an eternity in the Waiting
Room.'

*Adrian goes down on one knee in front of the
audience and spreads his arms out, Al Jolson
style, with a sick grin.*

ADRIAN
(bellowing loudly)
Ain't life grand?

KAYE
You must have had a great need for
attention when you were a child.

*Adrian hangs his head in exaggerated sorrow,
like a circus clown.*
KAYE
Are you sure your parents weren't
cousins?

*Continuing his mime, Adrian lifts his head,
shifting his eyes to one side, as if to give
serious consideration to this thought. Once
done, a huge, dirty smile comes to his face.
Suddenly serious, he hangs his head in mock
sorrow again. Kaye continues reading.*

KAYE
'Instructions for the playing of
the game: the players will find
before them a revolver and one
bullet. Before each play, player
will load chamber with bullet and
spin chamber.

Player must then recite a
confessional of truth from their
life no other person has ever
heard.'

Adrian looks up and off into the distance.

> ### ADRIAN
> Whatever happened to simple
> games ike Monopoly and Parchese?

> ### KAYE
> 'At the completion of his confes-
> sional, player must place barrel of
> gun to head and pull trigger.
> Should player receive a bullet
> through the head, HE will be given
> passage into Heaven, being raised
> to the next spiritual level.
> The remaining player will be left
> behind to play the Game forever.
> All lies will result in a forfeit
> of the game and an eternity in the
> Waiting Room for both players.

> ### KAYE/ADRIAN
> *(unison)*
> 'The playing of the Waiting Room
> game is the purging of secrets for
> the purification of the soul. A
> searchlight into the darkness of
> the heart. May this Game enlighten
> you to the nature of life.. and
> death.'

> ### KAYE
> You know this by heart.

Adrian gets up.

ADRIAN
I've had practice.

KAYE
How long have you been here?

ADRIAN
An eternity.

Kaye struggles to be sympathetic, but it's a stretch.

KAYE
That's hard to imagine.

ADRIAN
Tell me about it.

KAYE
I'm sorry.

ADRIAN
Don't strain yourself. Save it for
The Warden.

KAYE
Who is this maniac who thinks he
can run our lives?

ADRIAN

It's not our lives to run anymore,
Kaye. He's not a madman. As far as
I can tell, he's some kind of...
demigod. He's got a point to make,
but in making it, he's having his
fun, too. At your expense. And
mine.

KAYE

I don't believe in Gods, or
demigods, or myths, legends or
fairy tales or anything I can't
hold in my hands. I am a realist,
Adrian, and I don't believe in this
Warden or whoever he calls himself.

ADRIAN

You never believed in anything
Kaye. That's why you're here.

KAYE

You don't know anything about me.

ADRIAN

I know more than you think.

KAYE

What do you want out of this?

ADRIAN

(slams fist on table)
This wasn't my idea! It has nothing
to do with me. It wasn't freedom of
choice that brought us here.

KAYE
You're saying it's fate?

ADRIAN
I don't know what it is. But I know
I feel like a rodent in a snake
cage.

KAYE
Come on Adrian. This isn't for fun
and games. We're both here because
we both committed suicide. There's
got to be something in that.

ADRIAN
There's something in that, all
right. It means you can't even make
passage from life to death without
there being some major pain in the
ass involved.

KAYE
That isn't what I meant.

ADRIAN
How'd you do it?

KAYE
How did I do what?

ADRIAN
You know, kill yourself.

KAYE
Mine was a very courageous and
valiant death. I drank from the
poisoned chalice, died before my
kingdom's people, was carried to
the Nile. High on a golden
platform, I was mummified and
entombed with the pharoes inside
the great pyramid of Cheops. That's
the last thing I remember.

ADRIAN
You make a lousy liar but your
story is colorful as hell.

KAYE
Actually, I died a coward's death.
I took enough sleeping pills to
kill the Turkish army. I passed
from the material world with the
greatest support Phillip
Leaventhal's money could buy. It
was a Serta-Sleeper, extra firm.

ADRIAN
Damn. Talk about a cushy death.

*Kaye attempts some sort of honesty, but it's
tough.*

KAYE

I've always been a coward, Adrian.
Scared to death of being alone. On
the outside, tough and ballsy, you
don't get in my way? Inside just a
scared little girl. I've always
hated that fear. I never knew where
to put it. It was just always
there, like that monster in your
nightmare that's somewhere behind
you. You know its there but you
just can't see it.

ADRIAN

I know the one!

*She puts up her tough exterior again to block
the pain of this feeling she doesn't want to get
too close to.*

KAYE

But you don't get anywhere in life
when you show you have anything
like that going on inside. Which
is why I got wise. I got hard. I
was the toughest kid on my block.

ADRIAN

I can just imagine.

KAYE

What was that supposed to mean?

ADRIAN

What'd I say now?

KAYE
Are you trying to say that I'm not
a lady just because I show a
masculine side?

ADRIAN
I didn't say anything like that.

KAYE
Well you were thinking it.

*Adrian shakes his head in disbelief. He pauses
for a moment, then speaks.*

ADRIAN
Why'd you cop out on life, Kaye?

KAYE
Who are you to judge me? What
The hell do you know about my
life to talk about copping out?

ADRIAN
You had a husband. A successful
career. You had a family. What
more could you have wanted?

KAYE
How do you know all that?

ADRIAN
It comes with the territory.

*Kaye puts down the wall again. She fights a
painful memory.*

KAYE

There's more to it than that. All
the money and a mate and a career
doesn't mean anything.

(*trying to hold back tears but can't)*

KAYE (cont'd)

... I lost my daughter,
Michelle. She committed suicide a
month ago. She was only fifteen.
And I loved her. I miss her.

*It's awkward for him, but Adrian tries to
comfort her. He doesn't know how to be
supportive to someone emotionally, so he's all
thumbs when he tries to put his arms around
her.She allows this for only a few seconds and
pulls away.*

KAYE

Don't do that. I don't need your
sympathy.

Relieved, he releases her quickly

ADRIAN

Thank God for that.

KAYE

Listen Mister Poughkipsee or
whatever your name is — -

ADRIAN

To-pit-sky. With a 'T.'

KAYE
Topitsky Shomitsky!

ADRIAN
What's the matter with just plain
"Adrian?"
KAYE
I don't want to get too chummy.
Being alone in a strange room and
all.
ADRIAN
You don't have to worry about me. I
don't see you in that way.

KAYE
What way?

ADRIAN
You know, in a sexual way.

KAYE
You don't find me attractive? What,
you don't think I turn men's heads
when I walk by?

ADRIAN
Let's just say you don't exude a
whole lot of warmth and affection.

KAYE
Oh. Is that so? Well let's take a
look at YOU, Mister Adrian
Co-Pip-si.

ADRIAN
Topitsky. With a 'T.'

KAYE
In my opinion, you're a self-
absorbed egotist, a sexist, and a
psuedo-intellectual psycho-babbler.

ADRIAN
Psuedo-intellectual what?

KAYE
Psycho-babbler. You say things that
sound good but they don't mean
anything. Politicians use it all the
time. Well I'm not believing a word
of it, Mr. Adrian Co-Pip-squeek.

*Adrian looks at her like she's just grown two
heads.*

ADRIAN
You think I'm lying to you?
Making his up? I wish I were. No,
lady, this otherworldly scenario is
as real as it gets.

KAYE
(playfully skeptical)
Alright. I'll play along with your
little game. I don't have any
choice, do I? Did you say you were
a ... *(snicker)* teacher?

ADRIAN
A college professor. Published.
With tenure.

KAYE
La-tee-da! Professor, huh? I know
your type. You wear fuzzy sweaters
and elbow patches on your
courderoy jackets. You spoon feed
the empty masses your cut rate
ideas on what they should know to
make the grade.

In the end, it doesn't matter
anyway, because it's all about
satisfying your ego, isn't it?

Tell me, how many of your female
students did you seduce? Or should
I also be including the males?

ADRIAN
A bitter, angry woman. Angry at
men. Angry at the world. Walking
through life wearing armor and
brandishing a sword and never
letting anybody in. That's really sad.

KAYE
You think you have it all figured
out, don't you?

*But Adrian has struck a chord. She bristles
with annoyance and is clearly uncomfortable.*

ADRIAN
(softly)
What were you escaping?

She thinks about it.

KAYE
My marriage to Phillp Leaventhal,
certified public accountant, an
excercise in pure boredom. On our
wedding night we watched dirty
videos in our motel room.

ADRIAN
Sounds like fun to me. So what
happened?

KAYE
He fell asleep. Do you have any
idea what it's like being all
revved up with no place to go?

ADRIAN
Yes! My honeymoon night with
Ellen! She and Phil should have
Gotten together over ampheti-
imines.

Kaye starts crying. Adrian just stares at her.
She's has a hard time expressing pain or
emotion, so she's angry at the same time.

KAYE

I don't want to feel like this. I
don't want to be here.

ADRIAN

What were you really running
from?

KAYE

Nothing.

ADRIAN

I don't buy it. That couldn't be
the real reason. It was Michelle,
wasn't it?

*Kaye goes into introspective mode. It's a
painful memory.*

KAYE

People die. You can't control what
they do. They decide to leave
before their time and what can you
do? Except it isn't fair. She took
a piece of me with her.

The goddamn kid, what was she
thinking? Didn't she care at all
what we'd think, how we'd feel?
You give life to somebody and they
give you joy and then they rip it
out of your hands and you're faced
with nothing but pain.

ADRIAN
The same thing you did to Phil.
"Ah man. A tale of quiet
desolations."

*Kaye gets up, walks around Adrian, watching
him closely with cool intent.*

KAYE
You don't care about any of this,
do you?

Adrian is silent, not denying it.

KAYE
You sit here and I can tell you've
got your own agenda. I learned
how to read people in real estate.
You get to know when someone is
not really interested in your
welfare. So what is your game,
mister?

ADRIAN
The very one we're avoiding.

She puts her face right up to his.

KAYE
Are you really the Warden? Or just
a madman playing a chessgame
with my spirit?

ADRIAN
You'll never know until we
commence the playing.

KAYE
Okay mister. I'll play your game.
I'll play it right and I'll play it
hard, and when it's finished, I
want out of this hell hole. I want
to be anywhere but here, but most
of all I want to be as far from you
as I can possibly get.

ADRIAN
I'll drink to that.

*Kaye grabs the gun off the table, loads the
bullet, spins the chamber and places the gun to
Adrian's head.*

KAYE
Or maybe we can screw the
confessionals and cut right to the
chase. Maybe when I pull this
trigger you'11 be forced to find
someone else to play your sick
game.

ADRIAN
You think I'm your enemy, but I'm
not. You believe what you will. But
ultimatly. The Warden controls
it all.

KAYE
The Warden. The Warden this. The
Warden that. (yelling) well I don't
give a damn about the Warden!
Do you hear that. Warden? I just
don't give a crap! Hey Warden!
What if I shoot your little pawn
here, huh?

Adrian sits perfectly still and confident.

ADRIAN
Go ahead. Make my day.

*She looks like she's about to do it, but she
loses her nerve. She walks around the table
with the gun.*

KAYE
You knew I wouldn't do it.

ADRIAN
I know you don't trust me. But I
am who I say I am. I was professor
of english at a community college
in Brooklyn, trying to teach
creative writing to kids who would
only graduate to robbing liquor
stores.

KAYE
Well that is just SO interesting.

ADRIAN
They were mindless. Totally devoid
of any creativity. The least I
expected of them was some level of
literacy. Or at least an attempt
at writing down what they were
experiencing living in poverty and
hopelessness.

KAYE
So you should've TAUGHT them.

ADRIAN
You can't teach what isn't already
in the heart.

KAYE
(sadly)
I don't think I've ever felt
anything in the heart.

ADRIAN
I don't believe that.

She snaps out of it, putting her wall up again.

KAYE
Shall we let the Game begin?

ADRIAN
The Warden would like that.

She hands him the gun. Adrian stares at blankly before taking it. He stands up as she sits in her chair. Has to steel himself for the resolve to begin. He looks to the ceiling.

ADRIAN
We're ready to start. Warden.

There is no answer. Adrian spins the chamber.

ADRIAN
(continuing)
To plumb the depths of Adrian Topitsky's soul, eh? I'm just a polish Jew from Philadelphia, transplanted to Brooklyn for a career in broken dreams.
I tried the catholic church because I was trying to impress an Italian girl I'd had my eyes on in high school. I knelt through so many masses I've had calluses on my knees. So you could say I abandoned Judaism for the promise of love.

KAYE
For the promise of sex is more
Like it.

ADRIAN
Do you mind?

KAYE
Go ahead. I'm not stopping you.

ADRIAN

Thank you! It was then I found out
the entire structure of the church
depends on guilt and fear. I
abandoned Jesus when I found out
that the almighty dollar in the
collection plate. It was the only
thing that kept it all going. It
was the fuel that fired off
the engine of fear.
Believers!

ADRIAN (cont'd)

They are blind sheep being led
down the road of destruction!

KAYE
(banging on table)
Here here!

ADRIAN
(with difficulty)
So after being raised in the shadow
of the Church, I gave up on God. I
just ceased believing in him.

KAYE
So what is your confession?

ADRIAN
The cause and effect principle, huh
Kaye? That's the law of physics.
Well, let's call my confession the
result of the law of the jungle.
Topitsky's Law.

ADRIAN (cont'd)
Having given up on God, I figured
any action would be justified.
That's when I decided to throw
Stanley Stewart to the lions.

KAYE
Stanley Stewart?

ADRIAN
Professor. The head of the English
department. Damn good writer.
   (with difficulty)
He was my friend. I wanted his
position. But there was no way I'd
ever get it unless he quit, died,
or was fired.

KAYE
   (excitedly)
Did you kill him?

ADRIAN
Oh I killed him alright. I killed
him good. I took away his respect.
His pride. Everything that was dear
to him. You see, I set Stanley
Stewart up and sent him up the
river. I planted a few suggestions
with administration that he'd been
hitting the booze. Not entirely
untrue, since I'd take him out and
get him drunk. Then I arranged to
have a young female student of his
seduce him.

ADRIAN (cont'd)
She owed me a favor for bumping
up her grades.

They were in the motel when I
took the pictures. By the time I
was finished, Stan left town with
nothing. Even lost his wife. His
kids ended up hating him. I did
this to a friend.

KAYE
Why, Adrian?

ADRIAN
Because he was better than me. I
felt threatened by him. And I
wanted his job. I wanted the title.
And the money.

*Adrian places the gun to his head and slowly
pulls the trigger. Kaye REACTS with horror.
SOUND FX: We hear a loud "CLICK," then
there is a moment of relief, a few moments of
silence. Kaye gathers her resolve.*

ADRIAN
What makes friends do that to one
another?

KAYE
Greed. Ambition. A real estate
license.

He hands the gun to Kaye. She just stares at it, doesn't take it right away.

                ADRIAN
Your play.

                KAYE
I don't think I can go through with this.

                ADRIAN
The Warden is waiting, Kaye.

                KAYE
I can't---

                ADRIAN
        (angrily)
Stop your whining and take your place among the rest of us who went before you. Or don't you have the guts to face up to your truths?

She looks at him coldly. Then, defiantly, she takes the gun and spins the chamber. He sits. She stands, trying to gather courage.

                KAYE
It happened during the first
Summer of my marriage.
I was lonely. Feeling extremely
trapped. I was showing a house to
my best friend's sister, an account
exeutive at one of the studios.
She was an attractive woman. Tall.

KAYE (cont'd)

Dark hair. Dark eyes. Incredible
figure. I remember thinking I was
very envious of her. We were
driving up to the house on
Mulholland Drive. It was during
the day, during the week. The sun
was blazing down, and it was hot,
close to a hundred.

She sensed something was wrong
and asked me if I wanted to talk
about it.

I needed to talk to someone. I was
over the edge. I told her about my
marriage, how Phil and I never
talked about anything. That he was
too straight, too silent.
She had gone through a marriage
that had ended in divorce.

She was only in her twenties but I
knew she understood. We parked
the car and stood on the canyon
overlooking the valley and she took
my hand. Our clothes were sticking
to us, it was so hot.

*This part is really difficult for her. She begins
to cry.*

KAYE
And I remember that I didn't want
to lose control. I didn't want to
feel all the things I was feeling
toward her. I never felt anything
like that before and I was so
scared.

We drove to the house. Our hearts
racing, we entered the house. There
was no furniture, just empty walls
and floors and bare windows. I
remember her softly talking to me,
guiding me gently toward where I
knew I needed to go.

ADRIAN
I wish I had been there.

KAYE
There were no sounds but our
voices echoing through the empty
rooms.

She joked that it sounded like the
silence of the ghosts of people who
had lived there before. She made
love to me gently on the
hardwood floor and it was one of
the most satisfying experiences of
my life.

*She raises the gun to her temple and slowly
pulls the trigger. Adrian shows concern at this
moment, like he doesn't want her to get the*

bullet. SOUND FX: There is a loud "CLICK."
There is relief.

> **KAYE**
> Did I just see you show concern?

> **ADRIAN**
> *(quickly)*
> No.

> **KAYE**
> No. I did. Adrian Topitsky, you
> showed compassion.

> **ADRIAN**
> What do you know about
> compassion?

> **KAYE**
> Not a helluva lot. But I know I
> just saw it.

Adrian grabs the gun off the table in a fit of
angry denial.

> **ADRIAN**
> So what happened next? Did you
> see her again?

> **KAYE**
> No. I ignored her phone calls. I
> couldn't lose control again. I was
> racked with guilt.

> **ADRIAN**
> Why did you feel guilty?

She shrugs her shoulders.

KAYE
Why do we run away from the
things that set us free? It scares the
hell out of me. Aything that flies
in the face of convention. Anything
that has the potential to take away
the false sense of security that
bondage brings. It's a threat.

ADRIAN
It's why I committed suicide.

KAYE
(angrily)
That's no excuse! You should have
faced your demons. You left your
family. You had a wife and two
kids. You copped out, Adrian.

ADRIAN
Yeah, well what about you?

KAYE
(emotional)
I didn't have a family. I had a
dead daughter and an emotionally
absent husband. The least you
could have done was stuck with
your wife and kids, gotten a real
job, made some real money —

ADRIAN
What, you think teaching and
writing aren't honorable
professions?

KAYE
Let's face it, Adrian, teaching
high school and being a writer are
dead end occupations.

ADRIAN
Oh. I see. All the greatest writers
and teachers of our time were just
charlatans and bums.

KAYE
Well they sure as hell weren't
making any money.

ADRIAN
Money money money!! There's
more to life than the almighty
buck, Kaye. There's artistic
expression. There's the liberation
that the spirit of creativity brings.
There's helping other people!

KAYE
Where did all your writing and
teaching and helping others get
you?
ADRIAN
It got me closer to what it means
to be alive!

KAYE
And now you're dead.

Adrian gets right up in her face.

ADRIAN
Not inside I'm not.

KAYE
Touche'.

Adrian assumes the stance of a Freudian analyst.

ADRIAN
I suspect your problem is the
result of a manipulative father.

KAYE
And a passive-aggressive mother!

ADRIAN
That's really true, isn't it.

KAYE
(serious)
If I did anything far and away from
the accepted norm of conformity,
he would withold his love from me,
yes. But it's your play, Adrian.

Adrian grabs the gun and spins the barrel. It is difficult for him to begin.

ADRIAN
The subject concerns the killing of
my mother. How I was the person
responsible for her death. How I
pulled the trigger that finally put
her under.

KAYE
You killed your own mother??

ADRIAN
Five years ago she was wasting
Away in a cancer ward in a
Philadelphia Hospital.
Chemotherapy had ravaged
her. She had no hair. Her skin was
the color of cremated ashes.
An undertaker was the only thing
that would make her look better.
The nurses gave her injections of
morphine but the pain grew worse.
I tried talking to the doctors. What
could they do? Nothing.

The disease had transformed my
mother into this hideous,
screaming, tortured old woman.
Her only sin on this earth was to
provide selflessly for her
children.

ADRIAN (cont'd)
One night I bent down to her to
hear her whispering to me. She
was saying *(whispering)* 'End it.'
She was going against all she
believed in her wholelife. I couldn't
handle it. I cried.
　　(crying)
I took the pillow. I suffocated
her. I couldn't have watched her
suffer any longer. Oh God.

*Adrian stands off to the side, in deep grief.
Although it takes her a few moments, Kaye
awkwardly moves to comfort him.*

KAYE
Jesus. You whacked your own
mom?

ADRIAN
Don't get in my way!

*He angrily pushes her out of the way. He
places the gun to his temple. She rushes in to
try and stop him.*

KAYE
No Adrian!

*They struggle. He pushes her out of the way,
puts the gun back to his head.*

ADRIAN
It's over!

He pulls the trigger. SOUND FX: LOUD "CLICK." The relief is even greater this time. Kaye's relief gives way to anger. She looks to the ceiling. (to invisible Warden)

KAYE
(yelling)
What kind of monster are you?

ADRIAN
Forget it, Kaye. You won't get any answers from The Warden.

KAYE
(yelling)
You're no God. You're a demened bastard.

KAYE
(to Adrian)
What does he WANT?

Adrian laughs despite his pain.

ADRIAN
What does our great Warden want, our great demi-god in the sky? He wants us to purge ourselves of man's inhumanity to man.
He wants us to see our actions have reactions equal to their own weight. Welcome To The Karma Game! Let's find out what kind of Eternal retribution lurks behind door number three!

KAYE
I don't understand any of this.

ADRIAN
I think you do, Kaye. I think you
understand that when we decided
to take our own lives, we cheated
those we left behind. We tried to
clear the slate of assets and
liabilities by our own hand before
the debt was paid. And in the final
accounting, there was still a
balance due.

KAYE
I have a right to live and die as I
please.

ADRIAN
Or so we thought. But you really
have a responsibility to yourself
and the people who love you. We
failed to ride the bus to the end
of the line, to see what happens.

ADRIAN (cont'd)
Your family is still back there,
Kaye. They're grieving for you.
They miss you. They're in the
waiting room at Cedars-Sinai.
There's a possibility you might
still pull through.

KAYE
You mean I'm not dead yet?

ADRIAN
Technically. A silver thread is the
only thing that still connects you
to the material world. Do you want
to return?

KAYE
I don't know.

ADRIAN
Not many get a second chance.

KAYE
I'm afraid, Adrian. I don't know if
I can face them again. Their
expectations, their demands. My
demands on myself.
　(crying)
But I miss them. Even without
Michelle, I miss them.

ADRIAN
I miss everything. What do you
miss other than your family?

Kaye looks off in the distance, envisioning.

KAYE
Malibu at sunset. The way the
headlights of the cars wind up the
coast road at dusk. You can see
them from El Matador Beach,
heading north to their mansions in
the sky. How 'bout you?

ADRIAN
The sunrise over New York
harbor. It lights The Lady up,
cleanses her, makes her look like a
giant stone angel.

The tourists like ants scrambling
to climb her. Even the junkies feel
saved when the sun comes up on
that water.

KAYE
I've never been to New York.

ADRIAN
It's absolutely terrifying. Would
you like to visit?

*She pauses for few moments, considering, but a
slight Mona Lisa smile.*

KAYE
Yes. I'd love to visit.

ADRIAN
I'd like that.

KAYE
Can we stop playing this game,
now?

ADRIAN
Then we'll be locked in this dance
forever. A death worse than fate!

She reluctantly takes the gun, spins the barrel. She draws a deep breath for her final confession.

> KAYE
> I drove Michelle to suicide. She
> would come to me for comfort, for
> understanding, but I wasn't there
> for her. I was always running from
> emotional responsibility. She'd say
> "Mom, I need to talk to you. It's
> important and I'd say "Not now,
> baby, I've got to go. I've got to
> go to the office. I've got to show
> a house. I've got to go shopping."
> See, I was always terrified of
> having to open up to her. I saw
> myself in her, this confused,
> incredibly frightened teenager,
> wanting love but too afraid to
> show anybody any kind of
> vulnerability.

> ADRIAN
> Show your soul and you die.

> KAYE
> Yes. It was my father that taught
> me that vulnerability is weakness.
> And weakness is what the predators
> look for when they're foraging for
> their dinner. So Michelle
> discovered an escape from the pain
> of being human. That escape was
> Crystal methedrine. And alcohol.

KAYE (cont'd)
There she entered the darkness, the
funnel spiraling downward. I
watched her falling but wouldn't
catch her.

I could have been there, but I
decided to turn away because I
couldn't deal with it. In her
darkest hour, I was out trying to
close a sale. It was my fault.

*Sensing something about to happen, Adrian
tries to stop it.*

ADRIAN
It wasn't your fault, Kaye, don't —

KAYE
(yelling)
It was my fault! You're talking
about taking responsibility, lay it
on the line, well that's what I'm
doing. She would be alive today if
it weren't for me!

ADRIAN
No, Kaye, not this way. Give me
The gun —

She places the gun to her head.

KAYE
It's got to happen, Adrian, one of
us has to go in order to set the
other free.

*They struggle as Adrian tries to take the gun
from her.*

ADRIAN
Kaye, No!

*At the exact moment the LIGHTS GO OUT,
there is a SFX: LOUD BANG of a gun going
off. When the lights come back on, Kaye is
GONE. Adrian is distraught, crying, pacing
around where she once sat.*

ADRIAN
Kaye? KAYE? I didn't want it to
End this way, Kaye. I wanted to
Take the bullet for you. I would've
taken the bullet..for you.

He looks up to the ceiling.

ADRIAN
Alright, Warden. You had your fun.
It's time. We had a deal.

*He waits but there is no reply. The STEAM
AND LOCKS SOUNDS begin, as the door
opens, flooding the hallway with light as
smoke fills the corridor. The red light begins
flashing above the doorway.*

ADRIAN
No warden! We had a deal! We had
a deal!

*The LIGHTS GO DEAD. After a few moments
of BLACKOUT, a single spotlight hits KAYE,
who stands DOWNSTAGE RIGHT, addressing
the spotlight. Her face is serene, like an angel,
and she seems at peace. Adrian is GONE.*

KAYE
In a change as profound as can
occur when the cycle of life
delivers us from bondage, Kaye was
returned to Earth as a guardian
angel to help those who might die
by their own hand. She found peace
and solace in her mission.

The people who mourned her
mortal death found themselves
somehow comforted by an unseen
and unknown presence that told
them that she had gone on to a
better place, but was still, somehow,
among them.

The Warden decided to release
Adrian from The Waiting Room
shortly after Kaye left, but felt
Adrian's mission would be better
served in a place we'll call
Heaven.

KAYE (cont'd)
Adrian Toptisky communicates with other angels, teaches new arrivals, and often gets into philosophical arguments with authoritarian spirit figures. He is now working on the Great Eclisiastic Novel.

The Warden continues to watch over his dimension with dictatorial authority, receiving those who have decided to leave the material plane prematurely. He resides in a place where all roads to self-destruction end, where the journey to self-discovery begins.

All of us that have passed through his domain have been changed forever in great and far-reaching ways. We have all been touched by the place they call... the waiting room.

She bows her head as if in prayer, and as she does, the lights slowly FADE DOWN.

LIGHTS OUT.

CURTAIN.

Introduction to The Switch

This one act was first workshopped at the Stella Adler Academy in Hollywood, then later filmed as a pilot for a TV series that never got bought. It's one of my favorites about two African-American brothers, each growing up to become the total opposite of the other; one becomes a prison guard, the other a criminal and ulltimately a death row inmate. Their confrontation is the basis for the drama.

The Switch

Stage is dark but for the eerie specter of a battered electric chair at stage center illuminated by one stark circle of light. An ominous transformer type electric switch resides somewhere closeby, lit in silhouette in such a way as it will always be seen by the audience.

TWO MEN ENTER the chamber. The first one is dressed in pajama style prison blues and ishandcuffed. (For heightened effect, a chain attached at his ankles can act as leg irons) His name is BILLY JACKSON, thirty going on fifty, a murderer, manipulator, criminal and con man par excellence.

He is loose, unkempt and deceptively ruthless. He's got an attitude. A character description might be Fast Eddie Felson with two parts TedBundy. He is a talker, a man who could talk his way into the bank account of a lawyer or the bedroom of a nun.

He is outgoing, anal expulsive. He is led into the chamber by an armed prison guard named ROMAN JACKSON. Roman is the antithesis of the prisoner. He is also Billy's brother.
Roman is disciplined, a former marine, possibly in his thirties, maybe older. He is orderly, neat, and reserved. He believes injustice and authority. He is uptight, anal retentive. Beneath his cool demeanor is a perceptible anger that longs for release, a boiling cauldron of frustration.

Despite the layers, he is basically a likable man They enter the chamber, Billy freezes and stares at the electric chair. There is a moment of fleeting terror in his eyes, but it quickly flashes to his trademark smart-ass grin, the one he always uses when he's in a tough jam.

BILLY:
Oh gee, I'm real scared. This thing use batteries or is it plugged in?

ROMAN:
(pushes Billy hard into the room)
Just get inside.

BILLY:
I thought these things went out with the rack.
Why don't you just put me in boiling oil?

ROMAN:
My heart bleeds for you.

BILLY:
My imminent death. An eye for an eye, the
state rests its case against Billy Lester
Jackson, cold blooded murderer.

ROMAN:
Take a good look at it. Tomorrow morning
when they come to take
you down for the long walk, that chair is
going to be the last thing you see.

BILLY:
Why'd you bring me down here Roman?

BILLY:
You think I'm afraid of death? It'll be a relief
to be out of this hell-hole, a relief to be gone
from the day to day boredom of existence.
Let's cut to the chase, Roman. Why'd you
bring me down here?

ROMAN:
I wanted you to be faced with your own
mortality. There it is, take a long hard look at
it. Look at the man in the mirror. What do you
see?

BILLY:
I see one sadistic fool right now.

ROMAN:
No, reali-stic.

BILLY:
Come on man! How'd you pull it off getting me in here?

ROMAN:
I made a switch with Roberts at the shift change. He owes me. We got about ten minutes before Franks does his rounds. So we're alone, just you and me. I made sure of that.

BILLY:
You are one sick nigra.
Roman grabs him by the shirt and puts his face right up into Billy 's face.

ROMAN:
I should do you right now. You got no moral conscience, you got no sense of regret, and you're a burden to the state. Now sit your ass in the goddamned chair before I club you to death!

(Roman pushes Billy hard into the chair. Billy is grinning ear to ear.)

BILLY:
The Big Man. You always was this way,
Roman. Strongarm your way if you can't have
your way. Brute force as God.

ROMAN:
And you. You lied and cheated and conned
every person you ever knew to get your way.

BILLY:
Ooooo the almighty Roman Jackson has
spoken, the great authoritarian, the voice of
Gawwd! Jesus Christ. This place oughta be on
the cover of Medieval Times.

ROMAN:
(smiles, observing him)
That chair becomes you. Billy.

BILLY:
I'll bet it does. The equalizer of all things.
Justice in all its blind fury shall protect the
weak and fry the innocent, ey Roman?

ROMAN:
Whoo-hee! Listen to them quotes! You
learned more in five years of jail you ever
learned on the outside.

BILLY:
Damn straight. Lottsa time to catch up on my
reading. You ever read War and Peace?

ROMAN:
Hell no I too busy trying to keep your black
ass out of trouble. Not like it did any good.

BILLY:
*(raises his wrists with a pleading look in his
eyes)*
Take these offa me, Roman.

ROMAN:
It's against the rules.

BILLY:
Rules! All your life you followed the rules.
For once why can't you just loosen up for
chrissakes?

ROMAN:
Rules aren't for breaking, something you
would never understand.

*(Billy holds his handcuffed wrists up, an over
the top pleading look in his eyes)*

BILLY:
Pleeeease... Pretty please with a cherry
on top?

*Roman pauses for a long moment, then gives
in, unlocking the cuffs. He tucks them in his
belt. Billy rubs his wrists.*

BILLY:
(imitation of Martin Luther King)
Free at last free at last! I have a dream, that all the little childem shall be equal in the eyes of the laawwdd!

ROMAN:
Do us both a favor and shut the hell up.

BILLY:
Guess you could say my luck ran out, ey Roman?

ROMAN:
Your luck has run out all right.

BILLY:
What are you talking about?

ROMAN:
You'll see.

BILLY:
What are you scheming? I know that look.

Roman grabs Billy's wrists and struggles with him, finally strapping his wrists into the chair, and then his ankles, as Billy grunts and yells.

BILLY:
What the hell are you doing ta me you bald-headed bastard! Let me go!

Roman stands back, short of breath, he is both excited and scared, and there is a hint of maniac in him.

ROMAN:
How does it feel, Nappy?

Billy looks scared for a few moments, then his machismo returns.

BILLY:
You can't do this. I got rights.

ROMAN:
Yeah. The right to die.

The two men lock eyes. Billy begins his manipulation.

BILLY:
I am really surprised at you, acting like this. Have you ever tried looking at things through my eyes? Even for a second?

ROMAN:
Don't even try it.

BILLY:
Hear me out, man! The bitch was a tramp, she was begging for it! She would have given it to any loser that would've lit her glass pipe, and you know it.

ROMAN:
So you took her life.

BILLY:
I lost my head!

ROMAN:
You lost your head!! You dumb shit!

Roman walks over to the switch and places his hand on it.

BILLY:
Whattaya doing?? No man, don't
do it for god sakes! I'll do anything you say
man! I'm sorry.

Roman is enjoying this, he taunts him, pulling at the switch. Billy is struggling and screaming and pleading for his life.

Roman pulls the switch back up and steps away from it.

ROMAN:
Now that we've established who's in - "charge
- here, we're going to play a little game. It's
called 'Billy Jackson, This Is Your Life!'

BILLY:
Man are you crazy? What you trying to do?

ROMAN:
Wake up call, brother, and it's about time.

BILLY:
You're bluffing.

ROMAN:
Watch me!

BILLY:
You're serious.

ROMAN:
That's right. You know me so well Billy.

ROMAN:
I had to grant you one last request, you been asking to be alone with me for two weeks.

BILLY:
You never listened to me the whole time I been in here, you ignored every request 1 ever made this past five years rotting away in that stinking cell.

ROMAN:
I brought you down here to set the record straight. You've been a disgrace to our family. Billy.

BILLY:
Yeah right.

ROMAN:
Shut up and listen for once. You've left nothing in your wake but misery and pain from the time you entered this earth. You're a liar and a cheat and con man. I want to set the record straight before you go that you aren't going to escape this time.

BILLY
You never understood that it's life for the taking. If you don't take it, somebody
will take it from you. Or have you forgotten about our own brother?

ROMAN:
Don't you talk to me about Clayton.

BILLY:
That's right, Clayton! Clayton found out the hard way. There were three brothers, now there are two. Now he's dead, and I ain't playing the game like a chump, cause the kiss asses in this world lose.

ROMAN:
I'll tell you why I brought you here. I brought you here to face your demons.

BILLY:
I'm facing the biggest one of all.

ROMAN:
(laughing)
I'm not the devil, Billy. Your biggest enemy is
that ticking man inside of you. The two
headed dragon that can't be content unless
your manipulating someone for your own
gain.

BILLY:
You think you got the answers? You don't.

ROMAN:
Oh yeah right.

BILLY:
Check it out, Holmes. You work for the
system, you'll die in obscurity with a
headstone that says you lived and died a kiss
ass. Your wife and kids don't respect you.
You got no life. You're a walking corpse.

ROMAN:
Leave my wife and kids outta this.

BILLY:
Why you doin this to me, man? You still tight
'bout that hundred bucks I owe
you —

ROMAN:
Nix that hundred bucks. You're sitting in the
electric chair and you think I'm worried about
a hundred bucks? You ought to be put in the
dictionary under "dumb ass."

BILLY:
Why you doin this, then?

Roman sticks his face in Billy's.

ROMAN:
Remember the time you stole money outta mom's savings to go buy yourself new clothes to impress the girls in high school?

BILLY:
Oh come on. This is old news.

ROMAN:
Yeah? And later you did the same thing, stealing money out of her purse to buys drugs. Or the time you date raped Julie Rappaport?

BILLY:
Go ahead.

ROMAN:
Yeah, go ahead, where do I start? Why you do this to the people who care about you, what were you thinking?

BILLY:
I was thinking that nobody ever gave a shit about me, so I took what I could while I could! They knew what they were getting into with me. They got what they could outta me!

ROMAN:
Then what did you do? Then you turned you back on us. You practically killed momma with that little act.

BILLY:
Hey, so what, who died and made you God?

ROMAN:
You think I wanted this for you?

Billy laughs, a look of fond recollection on his face.

BILLY:
Hey, Roman, you remember the time we was playing baseball in Keppler's Feild?

ROMAN:
Yeeah. Every night at sunset, and Saturday mornings. We'd start the game when we heard the train going through Miners Comer.

BILLY:
The train was always on time!

ROMAN:
You could set you watch by it. If you had one.

BILLY:
How 'bout the time I hit a homer and it crashed through Fergie Reingold's
bathroom window, and he was in there takin' a crap?

ROMAN:
Well if he was gonna shit himself he was in the right place.

BILLY:
I remember you covered for me. You stood up for me. You took the rap.

ROMAN:
Yeah.

BILLY:
Why'd you do that Roman?

ROMAN:
Cause you were a three time loser even at six years old Remember pop said you were going to be grounded for the summer if you got into any more trouble?

BILLY:
That's right!

ROMAN:
Hey, I had a clean slate, so I figured I could afford a bad mark.

BILLY:
You did that a lot for me. I don't know why. I'd of never done it for you - or anyone else for that matter.

Roman thinks long and hard.

ROMAN:
That's right. You wouldn't.

BILLY:
Maybe you ought to try looking at things through my eyes for once. Try living in Billy Jackson's shoes for once. If you saw it from where I sit, you'd have some idea of why I am the way I am.

ROMAN:
See it from your eyes. You think that justifies you being a shit all your life?

BILLY:
I'm just saying sometimes you gotta put yourself in the place of somebody else in order to get some different spin on it. You was always smart, smarter than me. But there was places where you never been real bright.

ROMAN:
What are you talking about?

BILLY:
I'm talking about you always coming from a place of fear.

ROMAN:
Oh bullshit.

BILLY:
No, hear me out. You act like the big strong main, able to weather anything life threw your way. I mean, anytime disaster struck, who'd everybody turn to? Roman: a boat anchor in the stormy sea. But it's all a cover up.

ROMAN:
Okay Freud-black, so why am I covering up?

BILLY:
Because you're scared shitless. You're afraid somebody's gonna crack the armor, and what's on the inside is a scared kid. A coward hiding behind the mask of a hero.

ROMAN:
You don't have a clue. What the hell you know bout my psy-col-o-gy?

BILLY:
It's true! I read it in a book by this cat, Joseph Campbell.

ROMAN:
It isn't true at all!

BILLY:
Let's face it Roman. When you peel the layers away, you know what's left? A big piece of fried chicken!

ROMAN:
Don't call me that!

BILLY:
Yes! Fried chicken! KFC! Bawk! Bawk Bawk
Bawk Bawk Bawk Bawwwwwwk!

ROMAN:
Knock it off!

BILLY:
Fried chicken and a scaredy cat!

ROMAN:
No I'm not!

*The whole argument has escalated into a
childhood spat, two little boys calling each
other names. This is obviously getting to
Roman who grows angrier and angrier.*

BILLY:
Oh yes! Look at you! It's written all over your
face! You're a whews!

*(Roman grabs Billy by the shirt and shakes
him.)*

ROMAN:
Shut up! You hear me? Shut the hell up!

*Billy has won. He is looking at Roman with a
sick smile on his face.*

BILLY:
What are you gonna do, Roman? Beat me up?

Roman comes to his senses. He lets go, disgusted with himself.

ROMAN:
I should fry you right here and now!

BILLY:
Better yet, why don't you prove to me before I leave this world that you are a man of courage.

ROMAN:
All right smart man, how do I do that?

BILLY:
By putting yourself in this chair.

ROMAN:
Don't talk crazy.

BILLY:
I'm serious! Sit in this chair and tell me it doesn't make you feel different.

ROMAN:
I'm not sitting in that chair, Billy.

BILLY:
Of course not! Because you're afraid.

ROMAN:
I'm not afraid of nothing!

BILLY:
You are, man. And that's because you are fearful somebody else's might shake up your one sided little world.

ROMAN:
You read too much, that's your problem.

BILLY:
All right then! Unstrap me from this chair and you sit here and prove to me you aren't a coward.

ROMAN:
You're never happy, are you? You gotta have your way. All right! Dammit!

Roman, pissed, unstraps Billy.

BILLY:
(Smiling, rubs his wrists)
That's what I'm talkin 'bout. Now you're making some damn sense. *(gets up)*So you think you can site where I sit? You think you look at the world through my eyes?

ROMAN:
I don't wanna see through your eyes.

BILLY:
I got news for you, brother. You don't have no handle on reality. Cause life on the street ain't about kissing up, it's about hustle. It's about keeping money in your packet and your ass above ground. It's about staying one step ahead of the eight ball.

ROMAN:
Looks like you behind the eight ball now, cuz.

BILLY:
You wanna know how it is, man? I'll tell you how it is. When you got guys that'll stick it to you for five dollars. And while you are living and dying on the street, you have to worry about eating.

ROMAN:
You eat like everybody else, you get a damned job.

BILLY:
Who was gonna hire me? Huh? Who's gonna hire a man with an eighth grade education, two priors and a belly full of hate?
(imitating a lawyer looking at a job application)

'Uh yes, mister Jackson, we see here you have a drug record, prior assualts, a rape conviction, and a great deal of valuable experience as a crack dealer. When can you start?'

The cards were stacked against me from the start.

ROMAN:
You started with an even deck, just like everybody else. Problem is you never figured it was easy enough. Nobody owes you a living, you got to go out and make it on your own. Climb above the fray. Let your spirit shine instead of your damn ego.

BILLY:
The only thing that's shining is your fool head. You work for chump change and you end up a wage slave, just like pop. You end up sacrificing your dignity for a dollar, you want to live with that every day?

ROMAN:
Maybe you need to come down off the cross and start living in the real world.

BILLY:
You want to talk about real world living? You want to see what it looks like on
this side of the glass? There it is, man. Show me you got what it takes. Show me you not living in fear twenty five hours of your twenty four hour day. Do it man.

ROMAN:
You're crazy.

BILLY:
Go on!

ROMAN:
I ain't playing your games no more —

BILLY:
Because you are a bunch of talk! You lied
your way through life!

ROMAN:
I'm warning you. Billy —

BILLY:
Show me, just you and me, man, it's my last
request. Billy Jackson's Greatest
Hits. The seat of honor... awaits.

*Roman thinks about it, then backs into the
chair.*

ROMAN:
Are you happy, now?

BILLY:
That's great. You are halfway there. Now the
straps.

ROMAN:
Get outta here!

BILLY:
The straps Roman! Show me you are the man!

Roman straps one of his wrists in, Billy does the other, then does his ankles, and steps back. Roman looks truly helpless.

BILLY:
(smiling)
Now ain't this a Kodak moment?

ROMAN:
I don't know how I let you talk me into these things.

BILLY:
Well Roman I think I underestimated you. You have more guts than I thought.

ROMAN:
Get to it man.

Billy places the skullcap on Roman.

BILLY:
Gladly.

ROMAN:
What you doing?

BILLY:
It's 'lectric ladyland time, are you experienced?

ROMAN:
It isn't funny.

BILLY:
Hey excuse me, dumb ass, but I was talking. You don't interrupt me when I'm talking. Do you understand, your chumpness?

Roman glares at him.

BILLY:
I can't hear you!

ROMAN:
Yeah I understand.

BILLY:
Good. I'm glad that you do. Now that we have an understanding, I can give you a little more perspective, since we be talking about that. See, there's this world according to Billy, and that world was a world of wonder, what could of been a place of fairness. But you see early on in this world, I had this man trying to pull the rug out from under me, trying to belittle me in the eyes of my parents, my peers, and ultimately, myself. But you see, I persevered through this, cause the innocence of that childhood, of a happier time, an era was dawning.

ROMAN:
(*reminiscing*)
Yeah, those were the days, huh?

BILLY:
Damn straight! Man, it was the sixties in East
LA, the streets were alive, Motown was on the
radio, and a black awareness like no other
time in history. The sisters were out, fro'd out
and bodies swinging in the clubs. An era of
free love. Smokey Robinson playing out of
windows, cadillac alleys, card games at Mae's
and dancing in the streets. In that fateful
summer when the city caught on fire, when
all our dreams came to a close. The day the
music died, and the king was dead.

ROMAN:
Amen. And I thought Don Conmelius was my
lawd and savior. Make way for the
Soooooooouullllllll
Traiiiiiiiiiiinnnnnnn.....

BILLY:
Please Roman I'm trying to think.

ROMAN:
Well that's an impossibility in itself.

BILLY:
I found myself embroiled in the heat, trying
to make sense of what the civil rights
movement was supposed to be, and what it
had become. Yeah we was just kids then,
what could we do? It was our brothers and
sisters that were out burning and looting,
even our parents, running out of burning
storefronts with civil rights on their tee shirts
and television sets and radios under their

arms. But see, I made it through that, I survived. I survived when Clayton hadn't when they killed him in the streets, and when they beat our brothers up and left em half dead and bleeding in the gutter. But there emerged a different enemy, a giant of a man who was always looking in on my chess game and ready to kick the pieces in my face. A man who outdid me in every way, and when compared to him, I was nothing.

ROMAN:
Who was this great man? Somehow I have a feeling I know him.

BILLY:
That man was you, Roman. When our parents would say 'Why can't you be like Roman?", I would tell them, because I am not my brother, I am myself, with my own flesh, with my own motivation, and my own personality. But I would spend the rest of my life living in his shadow, trying to live up to an image I could never possibly duplicate, let alone outdo.

ROMAN:
You never had to live in my shadow. You had your own free will to make yourself whatever you wanted to be.

BILLY:
I was a victim. And became a sacrifice to the great white way.

ROMAN:
(yelling)
That's bullshit. You made yourself a victim!

BILLY:
(in his face)
Don't tell me about bullshit. It's truth, plain and simple. I got the short end of everything life had to offer. Everything!

ROMAN:
Oh poor me, poor me, poor me another drink!

BILLY:
Okay smart man. Well who's in the chair and who isn't?

ROMAN:
Well, you do make an interesting point, there.

(Billy walks over to the switch)

BILLY:
This is it, man! I'm frying your sorry ass right now!

Billy pretends he's throwing the switch, Roman is yelling.

ROMAN:
Hey! Hold on Billy, this ain't the way to end it!

Back and forth it goes, Billy threatening to pull the switch, Roman begging for his life. Eventually Billy steps away from the switch, smiling.

BILLY:
How do you like it, huh? How does it feel to be on your knees for the man? Well never let it be said I ain't go no compassion. At least where my brother is concerned.

ROMAN:
(sweating)
Man you got away of making a man's deodorant work overtime.

Billy walks over to him, pulls his gun out, puts it to Roman's head.

BILLY:
Or maybe we just do it this way. Make it nice... *(pulls back safety)* and messy. Maybe blow your brains out, and with em all the memories of the crap you pulled on me!

ROMAN:
Go ahead. Make my day.

BILLY:
You're changing your tune. A few seconds ago you were begging for your life.

ROMAN:
Yeah? Well maybe I figure you won't do it.

BILLY:
Really? You think I'm the coward?

Billy pulls back the gun, holds it out, snaps open the barrel, pours six bullets into his hand, throws them all away but one, reinserts one bullet back in the barrel, and spins the chamber. He places the gun to his head, and smiling, pulls the trigger. It clicks. Billy let's out a maniacal laugh.

ROMAN:
You ain't brave. You crazy.

BILLY:
No man, I'm just the baddest man ever walked god's green earth. I'm Napoleon, General Custer, and Superfly, all rolled up in one bad ass package.

Billy replaces the bullets in the gun, and slips it back into Roman's holster.

ROMAN:
You're a dumb ass nigra.

BILLY:
Is that right? Well who's the dumb ass nigra now, huh smart man? From where I stand and from where you sit, I'd say you are in a pretty awkward position right now, wouldn't you agree?

ROMAN:
So you think you know what it takes to be on top of things? To be a hero?

BILLY:
(in his face)
You're god damn right.

ROMAN:
And didn't you ever know the most courageous men who ever lived weren't courageous at all? They were just plain crazy and didn't care if they lived or died.

BILLY:
Well all alrighty then!

ROMAN:
When are you gonna get it through that peanut head of yours you can't win?

BILLY:
When you get it through that peanut head of yours you've been kidding yourself all along?

ROMAN:
Doesn't the word pride mean anything to you?

BILLY:
Well where's the pride in that? Pride? You can't take pride to the bank, and you can't use it for currency on the street. Too many brothers died penniless with their pride intact. Just like Clayton.

ROMAN:
At least Clayton had his head on straight. At
least he could answer to his conscience late at
night. Who do you answer to?

BILLY:
To myself.

ROMAN:
Yeah, that figures. All alone in a lonely
world. Because nobody can stand to be
around you. You're too selfish.

BILLY:
Hey I got ladies lined up to take a shot at me.

ROMAN:
They should build a fence around you and
sell popcorn. Hang a sign on it, says the
biggest dummy that ever lived.

BILLY:
You think people don't respect me?

ROMAN:
You mean those hoes that hang around at
Ozzies? Gimme a break!

BILLY:
They know a good lover when they see one.

ROMAN:
Let me tell you something, fool. If you had no money and you had no drugs, those hoes would kick you in the scrotums and leave you lying in the street. You know it and I know it.

BILLY:
They get their share, I get mine, that's the rule of the jungle.

ROMAN:
What about Eileen? And your kid, where do they fit into your illustrated jungle book of idiocy?

BILLY:
They don't understand me. They never did.

ROMAN:
Nobody understands you Billy. Not even yourself.

BILLY:
Roman, I'd like to hang around and chat a little longer, but you see, I have an appointment in the morning with the death man. But before I go, I have some unfinished family business to take care of. I want it to be known to the universe or whoever the hell is watching out there that in the final count, I got one over on your ass.

He walks over to the switch

BILLY:
In the end, all the philosophy and psychology in the world don't amount to shit, the bottom line is where are you on the food chain? And right now, you are definitely not on top. I know I got no chance outta here, but I do have one final card I'm playing. I'm taking you with me, Roman. You got over on me my whole life. Now it's time to right the score, to let you know that in the final play, you lost, I won.

ROMAN:
Don't do this Billy. It's senseless. I'm not the enemy, you are.

BILLY:
Too late.

ROMAN:
(yelling, pleading, till the game builds into a fever pitch)
Don't do it you dumb ass!

Billy pulls the switch, but nothing happens. He tries it again, nothing. Roman breaks into hysterical laughter.

BILLY:
What is this bullshit??

ROMAN:
(laughing)
I disconnected it. Billy. You see, I know you better than you think I do. I knew you'd talk me into the chair. And I knew you'd pull the switch.

BILLY:
The more I think I know you, the less I really know you.

ROMAN:
I couldn't trust myself or you in the same room. It was either you or me, and I
knew if I was placed in the position of killing you, I'd probably do it. And if you were put in the same position, I knew you'd do me in a quick second.

BILLY:
What??

ROMAN:
Blanks, Billy. I made the playing field even for both of us. Just you and me, little brother, on the chessboard of life.

BILLY:
I could beat you to death, right here.

ROMAN:
Yes, but you won't, because I'm your only ticket outta here.

BILLY:
What's this crap?

ROMAN:
Undo the straps. I've arranged for your escape. Billy.

(Dazed, Billy undoes the straps)

ROMAN:
That's right. Do as your told. In the end, you know your big brother is right

Roman rises from the chair, rubs his wrists.

BILLY:
How are you getting me out of here?

ROMAN:
(laughing)
Are you kidding me? We're the guards, Billy. We run this place, not the state, the warden or anybody else. We pull the strings. We write the songs that make the whole world sing! *(laughing)* Billy, you stupid dumm shit. Did you think I wouldn't take care of you, man? Blood is thicker than water, even the ice water that flows through your veins.

BILLY:
Your nuts. I can see it now, you've gone over the edge.

ROMAN:
No, man, I ain't nuts. Just a little crazy. But I know the meaning of loyalty. Loyalty to my family, to the people I care about, which is a lesson you might want to try learning. Don't say I never did nothing for you.

BILLY:
You're telling me you can get me out of here, how?

ROMAN:
At one o clock you gonna fake a real bad stomach ache, like your dying. And I'm gonna be there to take you to the infirmary. There's gonna be a trash truck leaving out the back of the mess hall at two thirty ayem It's a garbage truck. Billy, and I've arranged for you to be on it. Ain't that appropriate? It gonna come and cart your black-trash ass right out of here.

BILLY:
All this was a set up. You knew this all along.

ROMAN:
Of course. What you think, man? I'm a chump?

(Billy shakes his head in disbelief)

BILLY:
Why you doing this, Roman?

ROMAN:
Because we're family. Because despite our
differences, I still love you.

*The two stand facing one another, many
differences between them, but still one common
bond. They embrace, then pull apart.*

ROMAN:
Well, what are you waiting for?

BILLY:
(very moved, very humble)
Thanks. I'll never forget this.

ROMAN:
Yeah you will. You'll forget it the minute
your across the fence.

*They stand there, facing one another, there's
love, anger, hate, everything in that one look,
but we know they are bonded for life. They
embrace.*

BILLY:
Thank you Roman from the bottom of my
heart.

ROMAN:
Yeah Billy. From the bottom of your heart.

Roman reaches for the door, swings it open, then we:

BLACKOUT.

CURTAIN.

www.ingramcontent.com/pod-product-compliance
Lightning Source LLC
Chambersburg PA
CBHW071422090426
42737CB00011B/1545